MOD
SIGN
HANDBOOK

Fourth Edition

STANLEY HALL MBE
FCILT, FIRO, Hon FIRSE

Ian Allan
PUBLISHING

First published 1992 as *BR Signalling Handbook*
Second edition 1996, reprinted 2000
Third edition 2001, revised reprint 2005
This fourth edition 2010

ISBN 978 0 7110 3462 4

© Stanley Hall 2010

Published by Ian Allan Publishing

an imprint of Ian Allan Publishing Ltd, Hersham, Surrey, KT12 4RG

Printed in England by Ian Allan Printing Ltd, Hersham, Surrey, KT12 4RG

Distributed in the United States of America and Canada by BookMasters Distribution Services

Code: 1007/C

Visit the Ian Allan Publishing website at
www.ianallanpublishing.com

Copyright

Mixed Sources
Product group from well-managed forests and other controlled sources
www.fsc.org   Cert no. SGS-COC-005526
© 1996 Forest Stewardship Council
FSC

PREFACE

The third edition of *abc Modern Signalling Handbook* was published in 2001 and updated in 2005. Since then there have been various changes to the Rules and Regulations, equipment and methods, and those changes are reflected in this completely revised, enlarged fourth edition. Additional material has been included, and the use of colour has been possible, resulting in the publication of many new colour photographs and the clarification of line drawings. It is hoped that this handbook will continue to be of value as an introduction to the very complex world of railway signalling, safety and operations, as well as the associated Rules, Regulations and Instructions, and I am particularly grateful to Chris Hall for his help in its compilation.

Stanley Hall MBE, FCILT, FIRO, Hon FIRSE
Skipton
May 2010

Front cover: Three-aspect colour-light signals at the east end of Leeds station, controlling the departure from both sides of the island platform. Above the signals are 'Right Away' and route indicators. Below the main signals are position light signals, the signal numbers and telephones to the signalling centre. *Author*

CONTENTS

Above: Interior of Bolton West signalbox, Lancashire & Yorkshire Railway, 1912. The first electro-pneumatic system in Britain. *Author's collection*

Below: Interior of Horbury & Ossett signalbox, Lancashire & Yorkshire Railway. *Author's collection*

If trains always ran on time and never broke down, there would be little need for a signalling system. The timetable itself could be devised in such a manner that the trains would always be a safe distance apart. This was the philosophy in the early days of railways, and it worked quite well so long as trains were few and speeds were low; and even though breakdowns were frequent, the guards had time to go back along the line showing a red flag or lamp to warn the driver of the next train about the obstruction in front of him.

As the railway age developed, however, and trains became both faster and more frequent, the need for some system of keeping them apart — of preventing them from crashing into each other — quickly became apparent. The first signalling methods were based on a time-interval philosophy; trains were not allowed to leave or pass a station until a predetermined time had elapsed since the previous train had left, and the necessary instructions were given to the driver in one of two ways — either by hand signal or by fixed signal. Handsignals were given by a policeman appointed for the purpose by the railway company, and he gave his message to the driver by holding his arms in various positions. At some stations, wooden posts were erected, bearing various forms of movable equipment that could be operated by the policeman to give the various messages. These wooden post signals became known as *fixed signals* because they were literally fixed in the ground in a predetermined position. The first semaphore signal was erected by the South Eastern Railway at New Cross in 1841. Today's trains are still controlled by fixed signals, although shunting movements are dealt with by both fixed signals and handsignals.

The time-interval signalling system had fundamental shortcomings. As traffic levels grew, it became necessary to run trains at more frequent intervals, and if a train broke down, the guard had little time to run back showing his danger signal. A more serious problem arose when a train proceeded slowly for some reason and was thus in danger of being run into in the rear by a following faster train. This type of collision became known as an *overtaking accident*, with a meaning quite different from its use when applied to road traffic today.

It soon became clear that a much greater standard of safety could be achieved if a train was not allowed to leave a station until it was known that the previous train had arrived safely at the next station, and fortunately a means of allowing this to be done had just been devised — the electric telegraph. This equipment began to be installed in the 1840s, and it led to the development of what became known as the *Absolute Block* system, based on the principle that safety could be achieved if the line were to be divided into a series of sections (or blocks), with a policeman (or signalman as he was becoming known) at the end of each section, and with no train being allowed to enter the section until the previous train had left it. This principle was described in the following terms: 'The object of Absolute Block signalling is to prevent more than one train being in a block section on the same line at the same time.'

The term 'absolute' refers to the absolute prohibition on there being more than one train in a block section at the same time. The term 'block' then began to take on a more general meaning, embracing any signalling system worked by electric telegraph between signalmen in adjacent signalboxes, and it is still in use today to describe the system employed in the most up-to-date signalled areas, called *track-circuit block*.

The early fixed signals were operated from the foot of the signal post, but it was soon realised that it would be more efficient if signals could be operated from a distance by pulling a wire, and it became the practice to concentrate the operation of signals (and subsequently points) in one place, which became known as a *signalbox*. It then became possible to interlock the levers working the points and signals so that a driver could not be shown signals that conflicted with the routes which had been set. The first such interlocking was installed at Bricklayers Arms, on the South Eastern Railway, in 1843.

The essentials of a safe and efficient signalling system were now in place:

1. The concentration of control of points and signals in a signalbox
2. The interlocking of points and signals
3. Electric telegraphic communication between adjacent signalboxes
4. The Absolute Block signalling system and the regulations for its operation

The Absolute Block system was installed throughout Britain during the second half of the 19th century (its use on lines used by passenger trains was enforced by the Regulation of Railways Act 1889), and it was gradually refined by the adoption of a variety of technical measures mainly designed to overcome the problem of human error on the part of signalmen. 'Human error' is one of those phrases that over the years have acquired a special meaning in railway parlance. It covers unconscious or unwitting acts, such as a lack of attention or concentration, impulsive but erroneous reactions, errors committed under pressure, and just plain forgetfulness. It recognises the fact that human beings are not infallible, and that if the travelling public is to be safeguarded against the possibly calamitous effects of human error on the part of signalmen, it would be advantageous to adopt all the safeguards that the advances in science and technology can provide. These advances were almost always won the hard way, as a result of lessons learned from accidents, and the learning process continued at least until World War 2, but it was difficult to justify the cost of installing the complete range of safeguards at every signalbox, so busier signalboxes were better protected than those which were quieter and located on less important routes.

The braking systems in use on trains during most of the 19th century were primitive and inadequate, and as trains became faster and heavier, drivers found it increasingly difficult to stop safely if the signals were against them (*i.e.* at Danger). An auxiliary signal was therefore devised, situated several hundred yards before a stop signal, in order to give the driver prior warning of the need to stop if a signal was at Danger. This auxiliary signal became known by the term *distant signal*, and originally drivers were expected to stop at it if it was at Danger, but the impracticability of this was eventually recognised, and the distant signal came to be regarded as a warning or caution signal, giving the driver prior indication of the state of the stop signal ahead.

Many accidents occurred because drivers found themselves unable to stop in time at a stop signal showing Danger, even after they had been warned by the distant signal, and they ran past the stop signal

into collision with a train or vehicles standing just beyond the station signal. To avoid such collisions the notion of a *safety overlap*, set at ¼ mile, was adopted, and henceforth the signalman did not send the 'train out of section' message to his colleague at the previous signalbox until the rear of the train had passed such a distance beyond the stop signal. This safety overlap became known as the *quarter-of-a-mile clearance*, and the far end of the overlap as the *clearing point*.

The use of the ¼ mile clearance was unduly restrictive at some places, and a regulation was devised, universally known as Regulation 5 (because it was the fifth regulation in the signalling regulations book), which authorised the signalman at specified locations to allow a train to proceed towards his signalbox from the previous one, with a train or vehicles occupying his ¼ mile clearance. The driver was advised, by fixed or handsignal, or verbally, that he was being allowed to proceed under the *warning arrangement* (Regulation 5), and he was expected to approach the next signalbox cautiously. This regulation originally applied to both passenger and freight trains, but in later years its use was confined to freight trains.

The use of the Absolute Block system was mainly confined to double- and multiple-track lines used by passenger trains. As far as lines used exclusively by goods trains were concerned, a system known as *Permissive Block working* came into use, which allowed more than one train to be in a block section at the same time. There were no overlaps, and the driver of a train being admitted to a section of line still occupied by the previous train was advised of this fact either by the use of signals or verbally. He was expected to travel slowly enough to be able to stop safely if he caught up with the train in front. Lower standards of safety were accepted in the operation of freight trains than with passenger trains. Permissive block for passenger trains was often introduced at larger passenger stations to enable a train to enter a platform line already occupied by another train, but such movements were made at low speed and over short distances, and were therefore reasonably safe.

The development of signalling on single lines had progressed in a similar manner to that on double lines. At first there had been no system other than the timetable; then the electric telegraph came into use for passing messages regulating the passage of trains over single lines between stations. Misunderstandings led to several accidents, and the electric telegraph system was refined by adapting it to control the issue of *tokens*, which were handed to drivers and gave them authority to enter the single-line section. The tokens were contained in *token machines* kept in each signalbox or station, and the machines at each end of a section were electrically interlocked with each other so that only one token for a section could be out at any one time. Fixed signals were also used, and the system became known as the *Electronic Token Block* system, which is described in more detail in Chapter 25.

A system sometimes used on quieter single lines was the *staff and ticket* system. A box of tickets was kept in each signalbox or station, and could only be unlocked by a key on the end of the *train staff* (a wooden or metal rod engraved with the name of the section of line that its possession authorised the driver to take his train). There was only one staff for each section, and trains could only be admitted to a single-line section from the end where the staff lay. If a train was to be followed by another one, the driver of the first train was given a ticket and shown the staff. The driver of the last train through the section in one direction was given the staff. It was a cheap and simple system, but it could lead to delays if the staff happened to be at the wrong end of the section.

On single lines used by only one train, such as short dead-end branches, a very simple system came into use, known as *one engine in steam*. A single-line staff, usually a wooden or metal rod, engraved with the name of the branch, was the driver's authority to enter the single line, and as there was only one such staff in existence, safety was assured.

By the end of the 19th century, British railway signalling had evolved into a potentially very safe system, and henceforth its development was to be in a different direction. At that time, the railways had become very busy indeed, and much thought began to be directed towards ways of improving efficiency and reducing costs. The number of signalboxes needed was determined partly by the distance over which a signalman could operate points (finally set at 350 yards but less at that time), partly by the workload, and partly by the size of the area that he could control visually. One of the problems that existed in busy areas was the large number of signalboxes required in the conditions then existing. In such circumstances it was very difficult to keep signalmen fully informed of the nature and timing of the trains approaching them so that they could make the best decisions about the priority to be afforded to any particular train movement. There was often insufficient time for signalmen to consult one another about proposed movements, and the overall result was unnecessary

delay to trains on the one hand and wasted line or platform capacity on the other.

Fortunately, as had happened previously, a technical solution was available — the application of electric or pneumatic power to the operation of points and signals — and several large power-operated signalboxes came into use in the few years before World War 1. The first electro-pneumatic installation was at Bishopsgate, on the Great Eastern Railway, in 1898, and in 1900 the London & North Western Railway installed an all-electric signalbox at Crewe. Although the Absolute Block system was still used, it had to be considerably modified at large stations. In other areas, the use of power-operated points and *track circuits* (an electrically-operated train detection device) enabled two or three signalboxes to be combined into one, but the cost of such schemes limited their application. In Britain, track circuits were first used in 1894 in Gas Works Tunnel, outside King's Cross station.

Developments between the wars consisted mainly in the further application of existing safety devices and economy measures; but the birth of modern signalling, based on continuous track-circuiting, multiple-aspect colour-light signals, and route setting of points and signals by a single switch, with the interlocking being achieved by electrical relays, belongs to that period, and its development is the subject of our second chapter.

Above: Edward Tyer's single-line electric tablet instrument.
J. H. Edser

The landmarks in the development of signalling that we considered in the previous chapter might be briefly stated as:

1. The concentration in one place (the signalbox) of the operation of all the points and signals in an area, and their interlocking
2. The use of various block signalling systems
3. The application of power (electrical, pneumatic or hydraulic) to the operation of points and signals, enabling more concentration to take place
4. The invention of the track circuit, which detects the presence of a train.

In this chapter we take our story forward to the very latest signalling-control centres, known as *Integrated Electronic Control Centres* (IECCs), but they have their genesis on the East Coast main line at Thirsk and Northallerton, where, shortly before World War 2, the LNER introduced a new

Above: Banks of electrical relays — the heart of modern signalling until computers took over in the 1980s. *GEC-General Signal Ltd / Ian Allan Library*

system known as *route-relay interlocking*, in which the interlocking between points and signals was achieved by electrical relays, and which allowed the signalman to set the points and clear the signal for the desired route merely by turning a switch. On open stretches of line between stations and junctions the signals worked automatically, turning to red (Danger) as soon as a train passed them, then to yellow (Caution), then to two yellows (Preliminary caution), and finally to green (Clear) as the train went on its way and passed further signals. Three-aspect colour-light signals had first been installed, between Marylebone and Neasden, on the LNER, in 1923, and, in a subsequent development which allowed trains to operate at closer headways, four-aspect colour-light signals were introduced between Holborn Viaduct and Elephant & Castle, on the Southern Railway, in 1926.

The first daylight signals were installed by the Liverpool Overhead Railway in 1919. The District and Metropolitan railways had installed colour-light signals as early as 1905, but only in tunnels, as they lacked the optical power necessary for use in daylight.

The Thirsk and Northallerton schemes allowed signalmen to control a far larger area than previously, much of it beyond the signaller's view, and, in order that he should know what was going on in areas that were out of sight, he was provided with a large panel giving a geographical representation of the track layout, signals etc in his area. In the Northallerton signalbox a series of white electric lights on the panel showed which way the routes were set, as well as the location of trains (by red lights) and whether signals had been cleared for trains to proceed. The signalman had to remember which trains they were, so that he could set the correct route and give the appropriate priority at junctions. As the areas controlled from one signalbox became larger or more complex, a system of showing a train's description or identity on indicators in the signalbox was devised. These indicators were called, appropriately, *train describers*.

Signalboxes of the Thirsk/Northallerton type were known as *route-setting* or *one control switch* (OCS) installations, because there was one route or control switch for each route at a junction. A refinement of the OCS method has been the NX system, first introduced at Brunswick near Liverpool in 1937.

Above: The control panel in Hull Paragon power signalbox. It was known as the One Control Switch (OCS) system, in which routes were set by individual switches. It was brought into service on 23 April 1938 and was said to be the world's largest route-relay-interlocking system. *LNER / Ian Allan Library*

Left: The LNER had a very progressive policy for modernising its signalling. Northallerton power signalbox, using the OCS system, was brought into use on 3 September 1939. Signal N54 supports the following equipment (reading from top to bottom): route indicator for the right-hand divergence, colour-light signals, position-light signal, signal numberplate, white diamond plate (indicating the provision of a track circuit), and a telephone to the signalbox. The signalling was renewed in 1990, and the replacement signal a few feet beyond N54 bears a white cross, indicating that it is not yet in use. *Ian S. Carr*

Left: Cardiff West signalbox, with the points and signals operated electrically by miniature levers. It was opened in the 1930s in conjunction with the rebuilding of Cardiff General station.
Ian Allan Library

Left: York power signalbox was brought into use in 1951 and incorporated the Westinghouse OCS system. It had been planned by the LNER before World War 2 as part of its signalling-modernisation policy, and was said to be the largest route relay interlocking scheme in the world.
BR / Ian Allan Library

Right: Bristol East signalbox, equipped with push-pull slide handles, photographed in 1960. *BR / Ian Allan Library*

Right: Perhaps the ultimate in the entrance/exit (NX) push-button power signalbox — the Victoria Signalling Centre, which was opened in the early 1980s. This type of major installation has been superseded by the integrated electronic control centre (IECC), in which VDU displays replace the large control and indications panels seen here. *Marconi Co /*

Right: Interior of Saltley power signalbox. *BR / Ian Allan Library*

The letters NX stand for *entrance/exit*, in which a route is set by pressing a button or turning a switch at the start of (or entrance to) a route and pressing another button at the end of (or exit from) that route. This simplified the signalman's operating equipment and enabled the operating push-buttons (or switches) to be incorporated on the panel itself, leading to the very large combined control and indications panels that were developed from about 1960 onwards. These large panels required the signalman to walk to and fro to operate the push-buttons, and in some signalboxes the panel functions were split so that the signalman could sit and operate the push-buttons on a console in the form of a miniature replica panel, with all the signal, route and track-circuit indications being shown on a larger, separate panel.

In these later installations the train descriptions are shown on the panel by *train-description numbers*, each in a position corresponding to the actual location of the train on the track. Every train has a four-digit identity number, *e.g.* 1A20, the first digit representing the class of train (Class 1 being

an express passenger train), the letter representing the route or destination area (*e.g.* A = East Coast main line), and the second and third digits representing the serial number of the train or service. The train-description (TD) number is shown on the indications panel next to the signal which the train is approaching, and as the train passes that signal and proceeds towards the next one the TD number automatically steps forwards to be displayed in the next signal section.

These very large signalboxes became standardised during the 1960s and 1970s, and controlled most main lines and large stations. Technically there was no limit to the area that could be supervised and controlled from one signalbox, and natural development has resulted in some very large installations such as those at London Bridge and Victoria, each employing many signallers per shift. The name 'signalbox' was felt to be inappropriate for modern installations and they became known instead as *signalling centres*, although the designation 'power signalbox' (PSB) is still in common use.

In most large signalboxes using route-relay interlocking, the interlocking apparatus controls only the points and signals in the immediate vicinity. The interlocking of points and signals which are further away is usually dealt with in outlying installations, housed in buildings known as *remote interlockings*, each one dealing with a station or junction area. Communication between the main signalbox and the remote interlockings is by Time Division Multiplex (TDM) four-wire cable, either housed in concrete troughing at the lineside or buried at a shallow depth.

The basis of all power signalling installations is the *track circuit*, a simple piece of equipment that feeds a small electric current through a section of track that is electrically insulated from the adjoining sections. When the wheels of a train pass on to the section of track concerned, they short-circuit the current, causing a relay to operate, which in turn controls other operations, such as placing signals to Danger, locking points, transferring train descriptions on the signaller's panel or visual-display unit (VDU) from signal to signal etc. All the running lines (*i.e.* all lines other than sidings) are track-circuited throughout their length, and signals are erected at conventional intervals, based on the distance within which a train is able to stop from full speed. Each signal is capable of showing a red light, a yellow light or a green light. In busy areas and on busy high-speed lines signals can also display two yellow lights as a preliminary caution.

Track circuits have probably reached the limit of their technical development, and they are prone to *right-side failure* from a number of causes. Such a failure puts signals to Danger and causes delay. Much greater use is now being made of *axle counters*, as on the West Coast main line and in areas where track circuits are especially prone to failure, such as in wet tunnels and on

stretches of line affected by salt-water spray. Axle-counting equipment counts the number of axles on a train passing over the counting head into a section of line, and similar equipment at the far end of the section counts them out of the section. If the two counts agree, the section is considered clear.

The major development in signalling control has been the *Integrated Electronic Control Centre* (IECC), brought about by changes in traffic patterns and technology. The first one was commissioned at London Liverpool Street in Easter 1989, and was quickly followed by IECCs at York and Yoker (Glasgow). The pattern of train services today is much more stable and repetitive than it was previously, and is certainly more predictable. Passenger train timetables are now generally based on an even time interval between trains, the pattern being repeated each hour. Cancellations, special trains and other deviations from plan are relatively infrequent. Freight trains are not frequently seen on many routes.

A typical IECC is likely to contain the following features, which distinguish it from the previous generation of power signalboxes:

1. A stable and predictable train service pattern that can be entered into a computer
2. Automatic Route Setting (ARS), by means of which the route at a junction is selected by the computer on the basis of the train-description number of an approaching train and a certain amount of priority logic, previously programmed, thus relieving the signaller of repetitive tasks
3. Computer-driven train-describer apparatus, which operates the signaller's train describers and acts as an information base for the dissemination of train-running

Left: The heart of modern signalling — the computer and the VDU screen.
Author's collection

information, public-address announcements, the operation of train-departure indicators etc and also for record purposes
4. Several visual-display units (VDUs), which replace the signaller's operating/indications panel and require much less space
5. A change in the method by which the signaller operates points and signals; instead of using push-buttons he enters his commands either from a keyboard or by the use of a tracker-ball
6. The interlocking between points and signals, instead of being carried out by banks of electrical relays, is dealt with by a computer software program in conjunction with solid-state electronic equipment. This requires much less space, hence the IECC can be housed in a much smaller building than a 1960s/1970s power signalbox.

The role of the signaller in an IECC contrasts markedly with that of his colleague in a traditional manually operated signalbox. In an IECC the signaller controls train movements over a very large area, and he is able to do this because:

1. He can enter his commands quickly and easily
2. Automatic Route Setting lightens his workload
3. The visual information of trains, their description and disposition, which is readily available, enables him to determine priorities and make train-regulating decisions quickly and to the best advantage
4. Safety, which is a major preoccupation of a signaller in a manual signalbox, is largely incorporated in the signalling system equipment itself. In normal circumstances an IECC signaller cannot move points dangerously, nor give a 'clear' (proceed) signal to a driver when it is unsafe to do so. He can therefore concentrate on his train-regulating decisions without the heavy and physically tiring work of the signaller in a manual signalbox.

The stages in the development of signalling technology in the 50 years between Northallerton and the IECC at York have been as follows:
1. Introduction of the large power signalbox, with routes being set on the entrance-exit principle by push-button or switch
2. The incorporation of train descriptions on the illuminated diagram panel

3. Automatic Route Setting
4. The replacement of the large diagram panel by visual-display units
5. Computer-driven train-describer equipment
6. The replacement of relays by solid-state equipment for interlocking purposes

On single lines in areas controlled by power signalboxes, it has been quite simple to convert the electric token block system to track-circuit block; but in more remote areas, electric token block generally reigned supreme until well after World War 2. In order to simplify operation, however, a system known as *tokenless block* was introduced, in which the use of a token to guarantee that there would be only one train in a single-line section at the same time was replaced by a system of sequential track-circuit occupation and clearance to prove that a train had passed through a section before a further train could be admitted from either end. The tokenless-block system is described in more detail in Chapter 25.

Economic necessity led to the development of the most recent method of working rural single lines — the *Radio Electronic Token Block* system (RETB). It achieved its economy by eliminating the need for intermediate signalboxes and lineside cabling, since all train movements are controlled by radio from a central point. RETB is based in principle on the well-tried Electric Token Block system, the differences being:

1. Instead of the signaller handing the driver a physical token, an electronic 'token' is issued to the driver by radio, and appears on an instrument in his driving cab, the names of the ends of the section concerned being displayed in a window in the instrument
2. There are no lineside signals, merely marker boards, and all instructions to the driver are given by radio by the signaller
3. Hydro-pneumatic points are provided at the crossing loops. A points indicator (a yellow colour-light signal) is provided to confirm that the points are correctly set and detected for trains entering the loop. Trains leaving the loop in the opposite direction can 'trail' through the points without damaging them.
4. TPWS has been provided by Network Rail. A blue flashing aspect mounted on the stop-board post indicates to the driver that the electronic token has been transmitted.

British railway signalling is technically very advanced, and its development might be thought of as a series of steps rather than a gradual smooth process. And it is important to remember that, although much of Britain's railway system is signalled by modern methods, there remain hundreds of miles controlled by traditional systems born in the 19th century, together with a number of signalboxes that represent intermediate stages of development, although the latter are gradually disappearing.

It goes without saying that if the railways are to be operated safely, it is not enough for the signalling system to be modern and foolproof. It is also essential that the message given by the signal arm or light is observed, correctly interpreted and correctly acted on by the driver. The interface between signal and driver is vital, and the penalty of error is severe. Before the end of the 19th century several railway companies were developing forms of cab signalling to give audible warning to drivers and reinforce the visual message given by the signal. The North Eastern Railway pioneered the introduction of *Automatic Train Control* (ATC), but this was discontinued by the LNER after the 1923 Grouping. The only system that was developed and installed on a large scale was the Great Western's ATC, though the LMS had a small-scale installation of the Hudd system on the London, Tilbury & Southend line. Both systems warned the driver that he was about to pass a distant signal at Caution, and both caused the brakes to be applied if the driver failed to acknowledge the warning. After Nationalisation in 1948 the railways started to develop a modification of the Hudd system, which became known as the *BR Automatic Warning System* (BR-AWS). Installation started in 1958 and continued over the next 30 years, often in parallel with power-signalbox resignalling schemes. All the routes on Britain's railways are now equipped with AWS.

AWS is a fairly simple system, mainly advisory; and although it has been valuable in reducing the number of collisions, it has two serious drawbacks:

1. The audible warning does not differentiate between signals showing two yellows, one yellow, or red, which is a situation that could mislead the driver
2. AWS does not monitor the driver's response to a warning to see that he is braking correctly.

Consideration was therefore given in 1988 to the adoption of a system known as *Automatic Train Protection* (ATP), and trials were carried out on two routes from London (the Great Western and the Chiltern lines). However, the trials were prolonged and not completely satisfactory, and ultimately it was considered that ATP was likely to be too expensive to be cost-effective. It was therefore decided in 1994 not to extend the ATP system to other routes.

The abandonment of ATP left the railways no better protected from the consequences of driver error than previously, and it was essential that the defects of BR-AWS were remedied as soon as possible, in view of the passage of time during the ATP trials. A system was therefore devised known as the *Train Protection & Warning System* (TPWS). This system provides a *speed trap* on the approach to selected signals that can exhibit a danger aspect, and a *trip stop* at such signals. The signals selected are those where there are points and crossings at which conflicting movements can occur in the line ahead, or which have been specially identified as being at a higher risk of being passed at Danger. The speed trap has the capability of being effective at speeds up to 75mph, and is designed to bring to a stand within the safety overlap of the signal any train that it detects as travelling too fast to stop safely. The fitment of an additional speed trap (known as TPWS+) can extend the protection up to 100mph (160km/h). The trip stop immediately applies the brakes on any train passing the signal when it is at Danger. TPWS is described in more detail in Chapter 20.

The signalling industry, indeed the railway industry as a whole, is now on the verge of a major step forward in the long history of signalling and train control. European Union directives require the European railways, including Britain's railways, to adopt a common system known as the European Train Control System (ETCS). This has a number of features, some of them revolutionary, among which are a standard ATP system, the possible abolition of lineside signals, train position being reported by radio using transponders instead of track circuits or axle counters, and instructions to divers being given by radio. The Cambrian lines, which are at present equipped with RETB, are being fitted with ETCS as a pilot scheme. ETCS is described in more detail in Chapter 22.

PART 2

Chapter 3   Colour-light signals — their meaning

Colour-light signals convey their meaning to the driver in two ways — the colour of the light displayed and the arrangement of the lights when more than one is displayed. Sometimes the meanings are amplified by illuminated indicators, or by the lights flashing on and off.

Colour-light main-aspect signals are of three types:

1. Signals that can only display two separate aspects. Some signals can only display a red or a green light; others can only display a red or a yellow light, or a yellow or a green light
2. Signals that can display three aspects — red, yellow or green lights (but only one aspect can be displayed at one and the same time)
3. Signals that can display four aspects — red, one yellow, two yellows, or green lights

The word 'aspect' means the light or lights being displayed. Signals that can display more than two different aspects are known as *multiple-aspect signals*.

A red light means Danger, Stop. In normal circumstances a driver must not pass a signal displaying a red aspect (there are exceptions during failures, as well as in emergencies and when otherwise authorised).

One yellow light means Caution, and the driver must be prepared to stop at the next signal. In other words, the driver must brake his train so that he can stop at the next signal if it is still showing Danger by the time he reaches it.

Two yellow lights, one above the other, tell the driver that he must be prepared to find the next signal displaying one yellow light (or Caution if it is a semaphore signal).

A green light means that the line ahead is clear, and that the next signal will be displaying a *Proceed aspect*, which means that the line

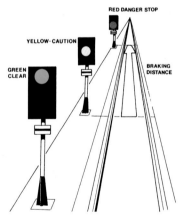

Above: Sequence of signal aspects seen by a driver running up to a red aspect in a three-aspect area.

Left: Three-aspect colour-light signals at the east end of Leeds station, controlling the departure from both sides of the island platform. Above the signals are 'Right Away' and route indicators. Below the main signals are position light signals, the signal numbers and telephones to the signalling centre. *Author*

ahead is clear at least as far as the next signal. A Proceed aspect may be a green light, or one yellow light, or two yellow lights.

The aspects described so far are known as *main aspects*, because they control the normal running of trains. The signals are known as *running signals*. The sequence of signals seen by a driver and culminating in a red aspect is as shown in the accompanying diagram.

Flashing single yellow lights and flashing double yellow lights are used in conjunction with the signalling of some facing junctions and are described in Chapter 7. A *facing junction* is one that can divert an approaching train on to another route, which may be a geographical divergence or a crossover between two lines, or just another line leading off the main line into, for example, a loop line at a station or a dead-end bay platform.

Colour-light signals are used both in colour-light areas worked under the track-circuit-block system and as a modern replacement for individual semaphore signals on Absolute Block lines. In colour-light areas all signals are of the colour-light type. On Absolute Block lines (see Part 3) it is normally the distant signal that has been converted to a colour-light. With certain exceptions, a colour-light signal on an Absolute Block line has the same meanings as the night-time indications of a corresponding semaphore signal.r

Train movements other than normal direction running movements are known as *shunting* or *calling-on movements* and are controlled by subsidiary signals. These signals are of two types:

1. Small signals located below the main aspects of a running signal. They do not have a Stop indication, because this is given by the main aspect when necessary. These signals are called *position-light signals*. They are unlit, except when required to give a 'proceed' indication.

2. Small signals located on the ground, usually about 6ft (2m) before facing points. The Stop indication is given either by one white light and one red light displayed horizontally or by two red lights displayed horizontally. These signals are called *position-light ground signals* (PLGs).

In each case the Proceed indication is given by the exhibition of two white lights at an angle of 45° and means: 'The line ahead may be occupied. Proceed cautiously towards the next stop signal (or buffer stops if there is no signal in advance). Be prepared to stop short of any obstruction.' The term *in advance* means 'in the direction of travel'. The opposite direction is described as *in rear*.

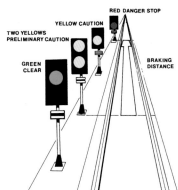

Above: Sequence of signal aspects seen by a driver running up to a red aspect in a four-aspect area.

Left: Two-aspect colour-light signal at Skipton, with route indicator and position light signal. The diagonally-hatched square plate immediately below the signal number tells the driver that he must telephone the signaller immediately, without waiting for the customary two minutes. *Author*

Where the position-light signal is located on a running signal, the red main aspect will continue to be displayed when the position-light signal shows Proceed, and the driver may proceed past the signal, even though the main aspect is at Danger.

When a main aspect shows Proceed, the line ahead is guaranteed to be clear at least as far as the next main running signal. When a position-light signal shows a Proceed aspect, there is no such guarantee. Any facing position-light ground signals intervening between two main running signals will show 'proceed' when the main aspect in rear shows Proceed.

Above: LED position-light ground signal at Grantham, showing two red lights. *Author*

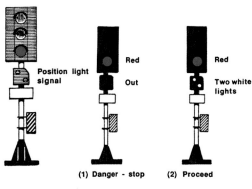

Position light signal

Red / Out

(1) Danger - stop

Red / Two white lights

(2) Proceed

Position light ground signals

Red / White
or
Red / Red

(1) Stop

Route indicator

Two white lights

(2) Proceed

Left: Position-light signals and position-light ground signals showing (1) Stop and (2) Proceed.

Below: The effect on the aspect of a four-aspect signal by the forward movement of a train

R — Train — G — G — G

Y — R — Train — G — G

YY — Y — R — Train — G

G — YY — Y — R — Train

Colour-light signals are divided into three types, depending on the way in which their main aspects are operated:

1. Controlled signals, which are operated from a signalbox by the signaller
2. Automatic signals, which are operated by the passage of trains and are identified by a white plate with a horizontal black stripe, fixed to the signal post
3. Semi-automatic signals, which are operated by the passage of trains but can also be operated from a signalbox or ground frame. They are identified by a white plate with a horizontal black stripe, and the word 'SEMI' above the stripe. The plate is fixed to the signal post.

All three types of signal change to Danger when a train passes them and occupies the next track circuit or axle-counter section (see Chapter 6). In addition the signals can be replaced to Danger by the signaller in the following ways:

1. Controlled signals — by the signaller pulling out the 'entrance' push-button on his panel (or performs a similar action in the case of other equipment)
2. Automatic signals — by the signaller pulling out an emergency replacement button on his panel, adjacent to the signal concerned. In the past it was not the policy to provide emergency replacement buttons for all automatic signals, but this has changed, and all automatic signals are to be provided with emergency replacement switches
3. Semi-automatic signals — by the signaller pulling out the ground-frame release
4. In modern signalling-control centres the signaller presses an 'all signals on' button,

Above: An interesting configuration at Birmingham New Street station, controlling train movements from both sides of an island platform. The letter 'R' above the green aspect has been illuminated by the platform supervisor to indicate 'right away' to the driver. *Ian Allan Library*

which restores all signals within a given area to red.

Signals can also be changed to a red aspect (or be held at red) in several ways without the action of a signaller or the normal passage of a train, as follows:

1. By the operation of a switch on the signal post of those automatic signals that cannot be changed to a red aspect by the signaller, or where there is no confirmation in the signalbox that the signal has responded correctly to the signaller's action.
2. On a track-circuited line, by placing a *track-circuit-operating clip* or a *track-circuit-operating device* (T-COD) on the line beyond the signal. A track-circuit-operating clip is a device consisting of two metal spring clips joined by a piece of wire. A clip is placed on each rail and this action causes the track circuit to be short-circuited. A T-COD is the same in principle but consists of screw-operated clamps joined by a thick piece of wire and is used to protect staff working on the line.
3. By the presence of anything that short-circuits a track circuit, such as derailed vehicles from a train on another line.
4. On a track-circuited line by a broken rail, provided that the rail is not continuously bonded (*e.g.* for traction current return purposes). A rail that is completely broken will interrupt a track circuit provided the track-circuit current previously passed through that rail. All track circuits require both rails to operate them. Insulated joints — opposite each other, one in each rail — are installed at the extremities of a track circuit. The length of a track circuit depends on several factors and can vary from 50 yards (45m) in a junction area to 1,600 yards (1,350m) in open country. In areas of 25kV electrification the insulated joint is in only one rail, the other being free from insulated joints as it carries the traction return current as well as being the return path of the track circuit. A broken rail will not necessarily be detected by a track circuit in 25kV territory, as there are alternative paths for the track circuit that can bypass the broken rail, using the traction return bonding to the masts that support the overhead line.
5. By a failure of equipment (usually a faulty track circuit or axle counter). All signalling equipment is designed on the fail-safe principle. Any such failures cause signals to change to Danger.

Colour-light signals are changed from a red aspect to a Proceed aspect as follows:

1. Controlled signals — the signaller selects the required route, and sets it by pressing the appropriate push-buttons or other controls. Provided that no part of the required route has already been allocated to another train, and that all the necessary points are free to move, the route will be set, and this fact will be confirmed in power signalboxes by a row of white lights on NX panels or by a solid white bar on VDUs, representing the chosen route. The signal aspect at the start of (or entrance to) the route will change from red to a Proceed aspect, being either one yellow light, two yellow lights, or a green light, depending on how far ahead the line is clear.
2. Automatic signals, and semi-automatic signals acting automatically, behave as shown in the diagrams. An automatic signal will change to a yellow aspect as soon as the previous train has cleared the safety overlap — normally 200 yards — of the next signal in advance. When the previous train clears the safety overlap of the second signal in advance, the automatic signal will change to show two yellow lights, known as a double-yellow aspect, which in turn will change to a green aspect when the previous train clears the safety overlap of the third signal in advance.

After a controlled signal has been changed to a red aspect by the passage of a train it will remain at red and cannot be changed by the signaller until the route ahead of the signal has been cancelled, either by the signaller himself pulling the entrance button on NX panels or by operating the tracker-ball and associated buttons at VDU workstations. The route ahead can also be cancelled by the operation of a device known as train-operated route release (TORR), which automatically releases (or cancels) the route as soon as the train has passed over it. Some controlled signals, however, can be set by the signaller to operate automatically. This is a useful device at, for example, a facing junction where most trains travel through the same leg of the junction.

This chapter sets out the principles involved in determining the following issues:

1. Should signals be two-aspect, three-aspect or four-aspect?
2. Should signals be controlled or automatic?
3. Where should signals be located?

The choice between two-aspect, three-aspect and four-aspect

In general, the frequency of trains determines this question. For example, on lines with trains at half-hourly intervals, two-aspect signals may suffice, with a signal every few miles capable of showing only a red or a green aspect, preceded by another signal acting as a distant signal, capable of showing only a yellow or a green aspect. When a two-aspect signal is showing red, the distant signal will display a yellow aspect. When a two-aspect red/green signal shows a green aspect, the distant signal will also display a green aspect. The two signals are braking distance apart, so that a driver travelling at the maximum permitted speed will have time to stop safely at the danger signal after seeing the distant signal at Caution.

Braking distance is based on the distance over which a train will travel before it stops after a normal service brake application has been made on a train travelling at the maximum speed allowed on the line at the point at which its brakes are applied. The ruling gradient of the line is taken into account in arriving at the result. Examples follow.

If the frequency of trains requires stop signals (those that can display a red aspect) to be brought closer together, a situation could arise whereby a stop signal is very close to the next distant signal beyond. It is unsatisfactory for a driver to be given a green light at one signal followed almost immediately by a yellow light at the next, and it is the practice therefore to combine these two signals in one signal capable of displaying red, yellow and green aspects. Such signals are known as multiple-aspect signals, and each acts not only as a stop signal but also as a distant for the next signal in advance. It follows therefore that the signals must at least be at braking distance apart, but not much further than that if unnecessary delays are to be avoided; the latter point is important. A driver will start to reduce speed when he passes a yellow signal, but the next signal, which was at red, may have changed to show a Proceed aspect at any time after the driver has passed the yellow signal, and he needs to see the next signal as soon as possible, so that he can take off the brakes and accelerate if it has changed to a Proceed aspect in the meantime. In practice, three-aspect signals are generally about 1 mile to 1½ miles apart, depending on the maximum speed allowed on the line concerned.

Where speeds are high and an intensive service is operated, requiring trains to follow each other at short intervals (known as *close headways*), a distance of up to 1½ miles between signals would prove too restrictive, and it becomes necessary to introduce additional signals; however, the braking distance cannot be reduced, so the driver needs to be told, two signals away, that he is approaching a red signal. The first of these two signals seen by the driver acts as a preliminary caution and will display two yellow lights; the second will display one yellow light. Since each signal needs to be able to display red, one yellow, two yellows and green, we now have four-aspect signalling, the signals being about 1,200 yards (1,100m) apart.

The braking distance determines the minimum distance between signals in three-aspect signalling, and between the double-yellow and the red in four-aspect signalling. A number of standards for braking

Line speed 125mph (200km/h)	Gradient 1 in 200 rising	2,140yd (1,957m)
	Line level	2,246yd (2,054m)
	Gradient 1 in 200 falling	2,455yd (2,245m)
Line speed 100mph (160km/h)	Gradient 1 in 200 rising	2,056yd (1,880m)
	Line level	2,232yd (2,041m)
	Gradient 1 in 200 falling	2,455yd (2,245m)
Line speed 75mph (120km/h)	Gradient 1 in 200 rising	1,273yd (1,164m)
	Line level	1,375yd (1,258m)
	Gradient 1 in 200 falling	1,511yd (1,382m)

Trains capable of travelling faster than 100mph (160km/h) are equipped with enhanced braking systems.

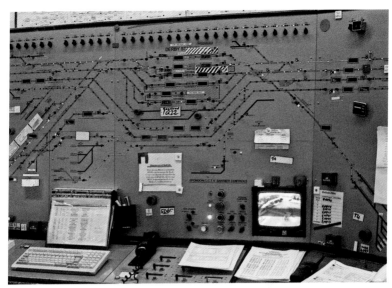

Above: The control and indications panel at Derby NX-type power signalbox (PSB), which was opened in 1969. The black rectangles on the panel contain the train description codes, and the row of black switches at the top of the panel are the individual point controls for use in special situations. The hatched areas indicate areas out of use during the station rebuilding, and the TV monitor shows Spondon CCTV level crossing. The area controlled by Derby PSB is being taken over by a new control centre. *BR / Ian Allan Library*

distances have been established, based on the type of traffic using the route. The following examples, *see table below*, are for routes carrying all types of traffic:

Should signals be controlled or automatic?

As we have already seen, automatic signals change from red to a Proceed aspect as a train proceeds on its way, but there needs to be some method of maintaining a signal at red at a junction where the signaller may have to stop one train to give priority of passage to another. In such circumstances the signal is capable of being maintained at red by the signaller, and is known as a *controlled signal*. Controlled signals are also provided where they protect a non-automatic level crossing, and in certain other circumstances. Controlled signals are capable of being switched by the signaller to work automatically, but continue to be called controlled signals. This automatic facility is useful where most train movements over a junction do not require the points to be reset, for example where a lightly-used branch line diverges from a busy main line, and at infrequently used crossovers between fast and slow lines.

Signals that protect points etc worked from a local ground frame are known as *semi-automatic signals*. They normally work automatically, but can be restored to or maintained at Danger by the signaller when he wishes to allow a ground-frame operator to operate points in the line concerned. The term *ground frame* (or sometimes *shunt frame*) covers not only an isolated crossover but also a former manual signalbox that has been retained to operate points and shunting signals in a marshalling yard or carriage sidings.

In all other cases signals work automatically and are so designated. Automatic signals reduce the signaller's workload and ensure that a Proceed aspect is displayed as soon as possible.

Location of signals

The positioning of signals is determined by the following considerations:

1. Signals are required where trains may need to be stopped, *e.g.* at stations and junctions.

Left: A fibre-optic banner repeater signal at Skipton, as an aid to the driver because the signal itself is round the curve. *D. C. Hall*

Below: A banner repeating showing that the signal ahead is 'on' (1) and 'off' (2).

2. Signals should not be located where they might cause trains to be stopped on viaducts or in tunnels, or halfway down a platform that is only a train-length long.
3. Signals should not be located where they might cause level crossings or junctions to be blocked by trains standing across them.

The location of some of the signals will de dictated by the juxtaposition of stations, junctions etc; the remainder can then be spaced at conventional intervals, bearing in mind the need to provide adequate braking distances. After a signalling plan has been prepared, it is necessary to consider the practicability of erecting a signal in each planned location. This duty is undertaken by a *signal-sighting committee* (see Chapter 24), which takes into account operating and technical requirements and the need to give the driver, as far as possible, a long and clear view of the signal. Where this is not possible, owing to the curvature of the line and the presence of obstructions such as bridge abutments, station buildings and platform canopies etc, it may be necessary to provide a repeater signal a short distance in rear (*i.e.* on the approach side). These signals are known as *banner repeating signals*. A traditional banner repeater consists of an illuminated small black semaphore arm in a circular frame. When the main signal is at Danger, the banner arm is horizontal; when the main signal is displaying any proceed aspect, the banner arm will be at an angle of 45° from horizontal. Nowadays the same effect as achieved by the use of fibre optics or light-emitting diodes (LEDs).

It will be clear that a certain amount of compromise is inevitable in the location of many signals, and it may not be practicable to erect

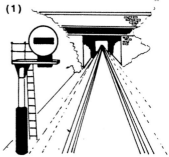

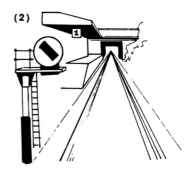

them precisely at braking distance apart, but they must never be erected at a smaller distance than that. The inevitable effect of all these factors is that signals may be further from junctions and points than is strictly necessary, leading to inbuilt delay in train working, or that they may have to be spaced out, leading to unnecessarily long braking distances.

In colour-light areas most running lines are fully track-circuited or are equipped with axle counters. A track circuit is a train-detection device (or more properly a device that detects the *absence* of a train) which operates by the passage of a weak electric current through one or both of the running rails. Track circuits are of varying lengths, ranging from a minimum of 20 yards (18m) to a mile or more, and each one is insulated, either physically or electronically, from its neighbour. There is no theoretical limit to the length of axle counter sections. Both types of train-detection sections are usually of a short length in junction and station areas and long elsewhere.

In principle, the electric current is fed into the track circuit at one end. At the other is a piece of apparatus known as a relay. When there is no train on the track circuit the electric current passes through the relay and causes it to 'open'. When a train enters the section of line, the electric current is diverted through the wheels and axles, away from the relay, which then 'closes'. It has been short-circuited, and the track circuit is said to be 'occupied'.

The track-circuit or axle-counter section, when occupied, performs a number of vital functions:

1. It holds the signal in rear at Danger
2. It locks facing points in the route
3. It notifies the presence of a train to the signaller
4. It can change signals ahead from a danger aspect to a proceed aspect
5. It enables the train describer in the signalbox to keep in step with train movements

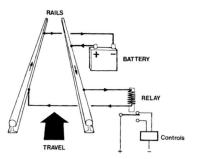

Above: The method of operation of a track circuit.

The track circuit has been the very heart of modern signalling, and only in recent years has the use of axle counters become more widespread. The track circuit was originally used as a safeguard against dangerous errors by signallers, who occasionally overlooked the presence of a train standing on the line near their signalbox and cleared their signals, allowing a second train to approach and collide with the first one. A track circuit ensured that a signaller could not clear his signals if a train was standing on the line and 'occupying' the track circuit. For the first time in the development of railway signalling it was no longer necessary for the signaller to actually see the train — the track circuit became his eyes. Coupled with the application of power to the operation of points and signals, the track circuit has allowed signalboxes to control train movements over large areas.

Left: Birmingham New Street NX-type power signalbox, opened in the mid-1960s to coincide with electrification of the West Coast main line, during which New Street station was completely rebuilt.
BR / Ian Allan Library

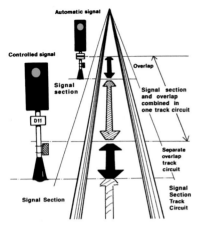

Above: The arrangement of track circuits in rear and in advance of a controlled signal and an automatic signal. A controlled signal will show a red aspect as soon as the first pair of wheels occupies the overlap track circuit. An automatic signal will not normally show a red aspect until the first pair of wheels occupies the track circuit beyond the overlap, because the two separate track circuits approaching and beyond the automatic signal are combined in one track circuit. This means that a train standing wholly in the overlap area beyond an automatic signal will not be protected by that signal, nor will a track-circuit-operating clip placed on the rails in the overlap area put the automatic signal to red.

Track circuits played an important role in the concept of the safety overlap, generally known simply as the *overlap*. In the days of semaphore signalling a train was allowed to approach a signalbox even though another train may have been standing on the same line only a few yards ahead of the danger signal, and there were a number of collisions and deaths through drivers' mishandling their brakes or not reacting quickly enough to the signal. In the famous words of one of Her Majesty's Inspecting Officers of Railways the safety margin at that time was 'the thickness of the signal post', but was subsequently standardised at ¼ mile (400m), although this may be reduced to 200 yards (180m) where the distant signal is a colour-light signal. The end of the overlap is the *clearing point*.

In colour-light areas overlaps may vary, but they are less than ¼ mile because the sighting of colour-light signals spaced at regular intervals is easier and more reliable than is the case with unevenly spaced distant signals on Absolute Block lines.

The standard overlap in colour-light areas is 200 yards (180m). Where speeds are low reduced overlaps are allowed; at 50mph, for example, the overlap would be 115 yards (105m), and at 30mph 77 yards (70m).

In the larger through passenger stations where an overall very low speed limit applies to all train movements, very short overlaps may be allowed temporarily beyond platform starting signals, so that a train can run into a platform while another train is leaving a different platform but converging on to the same line ahead of the platform starting signal. Such a *restricted overlap* requires the previous signal to be maintained at Danger until the train has approached close to it, when the signal is allowed to clear to a single yellow.

Track circuits and axle-counter sections on open lengths of line are arranged as shown in the diagram left.

Track circuits and axle-counter sections are used to control the signalling of trains into terminal and bay platform lines where a train may need to enter a platform line which is already occupied, and to prevent a train from being admitted into a platform line that is already fully occupied. To achieve this, two track circuits are provided in the platform line, and a second train is only allowed to enter the platform (under the authority of a position-light signal) only if the track circuit further from the buffer stops is clear. This is known as *permissive working*. If that section is not clear, only a locomotive or two-coach unit may enter the platform line. This is controlled by having a short 'measuring' track circuit immediately before the signal (see diagram below). This arrangement is known as *Lime Street controls*.

For a train destined for Platform 1 the arrangements are as follows:

1. If sections C, D and E are clear the signal will display a yellow aspect.
2. If section E is occupied the signal will display a position-light aspect.
3. If sections D and E are occupied the signal will display a position-light aspect only if the measuring section B is occupied and sections A and C are clear.

Axle counters

As noted earlier, track circuits have probably reached the limit of their technical potential and

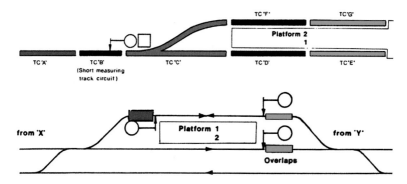

have several disadvantages. They are prone to failure in wet ballast conditions, causing signals to revert to Danger. Trains are delayed as a result. Rail surfaces contaminated by rust or leaf mulch may cause track circuits to fail to detect the presence of lightweight trains with few axles. Axle counters are not a new invention, and have been widely used abroad, but until recent years they were not considered sufficiently reliable to be used in Britain. However, they have now reached a sufficiently high standard of reliability and are increasingly being installed in new signalling schemes. They have also replaced track circuits in areas where the latter have caused reliability problems, for example in coastal areas and in tunnels.

Axle counters were installed at Glasgow Queen Street station in 1967 and on the Forth Bridge in 1978/9. In the latter case they were essential, as the rails were secured directly to the bridge girders. Subsequently the Scottish Region employed axle counters successfully for lengthy block sections where traditional signalboxes became fringe 'boxes to a power signalbox, as at Inverness, Aberdeen and Edinburgh Waverley.

Axle counters work on a very simple basis. At the start of a section of line they count the axles of a train passing over them, and a similar count is made at the end of the section. If the two counts agree, the section is assumed to be clear. They are not without their disadvantages. When they are being restored following a failure, or after engineering work, very great care must be taken to follow the laid-down

Top: Arrangement of track circuits into bay and terminal platforms, to allow a second train or locomotive to enter safely.

Above: Arrangement of short overlap at a passenger station to facilitate the use of the next platform by another train. A train may be allowed to enter Platform 2 from 'X' at the same time as a train is entering Platform 1 from 'Y' or departing from Platform 1 to 'Y'.

procedures precisely, to avoid the section registering clear while it is still occupied. Track-circuit-operating clips are ineffective (but the availability of train radio can render them unnecessary). They cannot detect obstructions on the line.

Although this is not their prime purpose, track circuits also provide a valuable means of detecting complete breaks in rails, which axle counters are unable to do; however, this protection is only partial on overhead electrified lines, which use only one rail for track-circuit purposes, the other rail being used for traction return currents. With the use of axle counters permanent-way engineers must consider how to detect broken rails by other means — *e.g.* increased inspections — if track circuits are removed. The use of axle-counter sections allows the removal of a large number of insulated rail joints required to separate track-circuit sections; this is a big advantage, removing a potential area of weakness in the track.

The term *junction* refers to any set of facing points in the normal direction of running. It covers not only a geographical junction, where the line splits off into two different directions, but also a track layout where the facing points give access to a parallel running line, or to a diverging platform line at a station.

The signals that drivers see when approaching facing junctions have additional roles to play, besides telling the drivers whether the line ahead is clear or not. These additional roles are:

1. To inform the driver which way the junction is set
2. To ensure that the driver reduces speed as necessary when the junction is set for a diverging route where the degree of curvature in the points and beyond demands the imposition of a speed limit; this is known as *approach control*
3. To ensure that the points cannot move when the junction signal is displaying a proceed aspect

These aims are achieved as set out below.

Informing the driver

There are three methods of informing the driver as to which way the junction is set:

1. By providing a position-light junction indicator, normally located above the junction signal, which indicates the route by displaying a line of white lights, either to the right or left. It is designed to be readable (*i.e.* the indications displayed can be identified by drivers) up to a distance of 750 yards (800m). No route indication is given for the highest-speed route, except that where there is no obvious main route a junction indicator will be provided for all routes. Where there are routes of equal speed, a junction indicator may be provided for each route. Where the track layout through the switches and crossings straight ahead appears to the driver to be a legitimate route, but actually leads to an unsignalled route, a junction indicator will be provided for all signalled routes.

Above: Junction signal at Exeter St Davids, with five-row junction indicator. *Author*

Right: King's Cross NX-type power signalbox in 1977. It controls 83 route miles of track. *BR / Ian Allan Library*

Approach control and release of the junction signal

There are several ways of implementing approach control and controlling the release of the junction signal.

(i) Approach control from red

Except where the difference in maximum permitted speed between the main route and the turnout at the points to the diverging route is 10mph (16km/h) or lower, the junction signal is held at red for a period when the points are set for the diverging route, to ensure that the driver receives Caution aspects at the preceding signals and reduces the speed of the train so that the lower-speed divergence can be traversed safely. In most cases, junction signals are approach-released from red, and this may take effect at any time after the approaching train has passed the overlap of the previous signal, subject to the following provisos:

1. The Proceed aspect at the junction signal must not become visible to the driver before he can see the junction indicator (for example, where the junction signal is beyond an overbridge which restricts the view of the junction indicator). To avoid misleading the driver into thinking he is being signalled along the straight route and consequently travelling too fast when he finally sees the junction indicator, the junction signal must be held at red until the junction indicator is visible.
2. Wherever possible, approach release should take effect before the driver can see the signal.

2. By providing a standard alpha-numeric route indicator on the same post as the junction signal, capable of being read by drivers up to a distance of 280 yards (250m). An indication must be provided for all routes except where the highest-speed route exceeds 60mph (97km/h).
3. By offsetting the signal for the diverging route to one side of the running signal. (For example a *splitting distant* signal.)

The arrangements for junction signalling are complex, leading to many variations depending on the local conditions, the approach speed, the speed of the divergence and how important it is to avoid inadvertent misrouteing of a train.

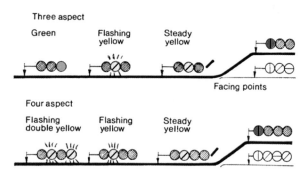

Three aspect

Green — Flashing yellow — Steady yellow

Facing points

Four aspect

Flashing double yellow — Flashing yellow — Steady yellow

Left: Sequence of aspects seen by the driver at a junction provided with flashing yellow signalling.

Above: Motorised points with secondary 'back drive' at Derby. The points lock and detection are contained in one of the equipment boxes at the foot of the ramp. *Author*

(ii) Approach release from yellow

A variation of approach control from red is the less-common approach control from yellow, sometimes referred to as a *free yellow*. The difference in speed between the diverging route and the highest-speed route (which should not be more than 60mph) should be greater than 10mph but not more than 30mph. The diverging route should be close enough beyond the signal that a driver driving, as if proceeding on the highest-speed route, does not have to brake further to obey the divergence speed. The signal before the junction signal must be able to show a double-yellow aspect.

(iii) Flashing yellow aspects

Where the diverging junction has been specially laid to allow higher speeds, and where approach release from red would not allow the planned speed through the diverging junction to be achieved, the junction signal may display an unrestricted yellow aspect to the highest-speed diverging route, with the previous signal displaying a flashing yellow aspect. In four-aspect territory, the signal before that will display two flashing yellows. The junction signal itself is released in the same manner as for approach release from red. Where there are successive junctions, and both are suitable for flashing

yellow signalling, it may only be applied to one of the junctions.

The driver must remember not only that a single flashing yellow light means that the junction ahead has been set for the highest-speed diverging route but also that it may indicate a preliminary caution because the next signal but one is at Danger. If the line ahead is clear, however, the driver will see the following sequence of signals in four-aspect territory:

1. Two flashing yellow lights
2. One flashing yellow light
3. A steady yellow light at the junction signal, changing to green (depending on sighting conditions, the junction signal may already be at green when it comes within the driver's sight).

Splitting distants

At certain junctions where other forms of junction signalling are not appropriate, for example at very high-speed junctions and at successive high-speed junctions, splitting distants may be provided at the signal in rear of the junction signal, and where necessary also at the signal in rear of that. These take the form of additional green and yellow heads offset from the main signal heads. The junction signal will not be subject to approach release.

Preliminary Route Indicators

An indicator known as a *Preliminary Route Indicator* (PRI), showing a white arrow pointing in the same direction as the junction indicator, or straight ahead if the junction indicator is not lit, may be used where it is essential that a driver is given advance warning of a diverging route where an unsafe situation could occur if the signaller incorrectly routed a train in a direction that would be unexpected by the driver; otherwise an electrically hauled train could be diverted on to a non-electrified line, or a train could come to a stand across a junction, causing operational problems. The purpose of PRIs therefore is to enable a driver to brake a train to a stand before reaching the junction signal if he realises that the route has been set incorrectly.

PRIs may only be used where the junction signal is normally cleared as soon as the diverging route is set (*i.e.* no approach control, no approach control from yellow with double yellow aspect in rear, and no approach control from yellow preceded by flashing aspects).

Where necessary, a PRI must be positioned beyond but close to any signal before the junction signal that would show a more restrictive aspect than that for the normal junction sequence if the junction signal was at red. Where the signalling is four-aspect, the number of PRIs fitted (one or two) depends on the speed of the junction — only one is necessary at a lower-speed junction.

Splitting banner repeating signals

Where a junction signal that requires a banner repeating signal has one or more routes preceded by flashing aspects, splitting distants or a double-yellow aspect (*i.e.* approach control from yellow), a splitting banner repeating signal must be provided instead of a single banner. The banner head for the diverging route must be fitted lower than the one for the main route, and must not clear until the junction signal has cleared for the diverging route.

Temporary speed restriction on diverging route

Where there is a temporary speed restriction on a diverging route, it is essential that drivers know which way the junction points are set, so that they

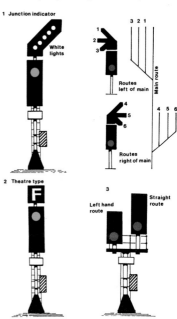

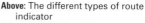

Above: The different types of route indicator
(1) a row of white lights,
(2) multi-lamp or similar, and
(3) offset signal at lower level for diverging route.

PRI warning of
Junction Indicator
in Position 1 ahead

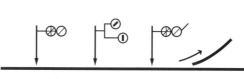

Use of splitting banner repeater indicating diverging route

31

can reduce speed as necessary for the temporary speed restriction. Therefore, where the junction is normally signalled to allow for higher speeds, a temporary approach release from red arrangement must be applied to hold the junction signal at red until the route indication is readable by the driver.

Approach locking of points

The purpose of approach locking is to prevent a route ahead of a signal from being changed once the driver has seen a proceed aspect at the junction signal (or a green aspect two signals away, or a double-yellow aspect at the previous signal). However, provision is made for the locking to be released provided that, if the junction signal is replaced to Danger, sufficient time has elapsed either for the train to have come to a stand at the junction signal, or to have run past it on to track circuits that lock the points.

Approach locking becomes operative immediately a proceed aspect has been displayed at the junction signal. It is released in the following ways:

1. When the train passes the signal
2. By the operation of a time release, which is generally between one and four minutes depending on the distance between signals, the type of traffic on the line concerned (passenger only, or mixed traffic), and the nature of the location (*e.g.* a major station or critical junction)
3. By a system known as *comprehensive approach locking*, which detects whether there is any train approaching a point from which the driver would see a change of aspect by the replacement of a signal to red; this facilitates a quicker release of approach locking but adds to the complexity of the circuitry

Also worthy of mention are some other items regarding points:

1. A junction signal must not be more than 880 yards (800m) from the facing points (or the first of a series).
2. Flank protection may be provided at junctions to protect a train from another train that is also approaching the junction and may have run past a signal at Danger (*see diagram below*). Before signal 2 can be cleared points Y must be set towards C to protect a train proceeding from C to B from another that intends to proceed from B to A and may wrongly have passed signal 1 at Danger. In more complex layouts it is preferable for an overrunning train to be diverted onto a line used predominantly by trains running in the same direction.
3. If a driver finds that a junction signal has been cleared for the wrong route, or if he receives flashing yellow aspects when he is expecting to proceed along the highest-speed route, or if he receives clear signals at signals in rear of a junction at which he is expecting to be diverted, he must stop at the junction signal if it is possible and safe to do so, and speak to the signaller. If PRIs are fitted (see above) they should enable the driver to stop at the junction signal.

The complexity of junction signalling arrangements

The signalling arrangements for the safe working of trains through diverging junctions where a reduction of speed is necessary have become increasingly complex as design speeds through diverging junctions have increased in response to the competing needs for faster journey times and increased line capacity. The arrangements set out in this chapter are intended to allow the designed speed of the junction to be achieved safely, and this is done through controls on the signalling so that safety is assured even if the driver should make an error. Flashing yellow aspects are sometimes provided to allow the design speed of the turnout to be achieved.

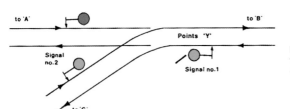

Left: An example of flank protection at a double junction.

The large power signalboxes using route-relay interlocking that still control many main lines in Britain were mostly brought into use in the 1960s and 1970s. Generally speaking, the technical equipment is housed on the ground floor or lower floors, whilst the operating room is located on the upper floor.

The most distinctive feature of the operating room is the control panel, which usually occupies the full length of one side, or may even be horseshoe-shaped. The panel displays a geographical representation of all the lines controlled from the signalbox, and contains all the operating switches and buttons for use by the signallers, of whom there may be any number from two to a dozen or more. Behind the signallers are a number of desks for train regulators, supervisors, announcers and assistants.

The signaller's role is to set the routes for trains, and clear the signals, in accordance with the timetable, and when trains run late it is his job to minimise the effect of such late running. He therefore needs to know about trains approaching his area of control so that he can make the most appropriate regulating decisions, and he can see where all trains are by looking at the control panel.

In order to set a route and clear the signals for a train, the signaller presses the entrance button alongside the first controlled signal on his control panel. The button then shows a white flashing light. He then presses the exit button at the next controlled signal along the route to be taken by the approaching train (one button normally serves as both an entrance and an exit button). If the

route is available (i.e. has not been 'promised' to another train), all the points are switched to their appropriate position, and locked, for the safety of the train, and if all the track circuits concerned are clear, the first controlled signal changes to a Proceed aspect. The signal indication on the control panel shows a green light irrespective of whether the lineside signal itself is showing green, one yellow or two yellows. A row of white lights is displayed on the control panel along the route concerned to confirm to the signaller that it has been successfully set. The signaller then repeats the procedure further along the route to be taken by the train until the whole of the route within the signaller's area of control has been set.

When the train enters the route concerned and occupies the first track circuit, its presence is indicated to the signaller by a number of red lights on the line on his control panel, and as the train moves along and occupies and subsequently clears further track circuits, the row of red lights on the control panel steps along accordingly, so that the signaller can always tell which track circuit is being occupied by the train. He cannot normally tell exactly where the train is if only one track circuit is showing occupied, but if two are showing occupied it is a fair deduction that the train is straddling the boundary between them.

As the train proceeds on its way the signals will change to Danger behind it, but the row of white route lights remains on the control panel until either the signaller cancels the route by pulling out the entrance button or they are extinguished by the automatic operation of train-

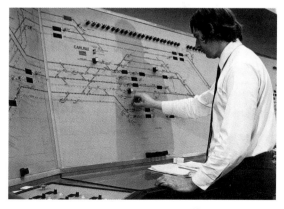

Left: A close-up view of the control and indications panel inside Carlisle signalbox, which was opened in 1973. *BR / Ian Allan Library*

Above left and above right: An 'OFF' indicator at Liverpool Street station, which tells station staff and the train guard that the signal has been cleared for the train to depart. Station staff may now indicate to the guard that station duties have been completed, and the guard will indicate that the 'right away' (RA) button may now be pressed. This will cause a letter 'R' to be illuminated on the signal post, giving the driver permission to start the train. It will not illuminate until the signal shows 'Proceed'. The other buttons on the post are (from the top) 'Train Ready to Start', which sends the message to the signaller, 'Barrier Bell', which tells the ticket barrier staff to close the barrier, and 'CD', which tells the guard to close the doors, if the train has power-operated doors. *Both D. C. Hall*

operated route release equipment, which is provided where it is reasonable to do so.

To enable the signaller to carry out his regulating duties he needs to know the identity of trains. Every train in the timetable has a four-character identity number (see Chapter 2), and its number is displayed on the control panel in windows or berths along the route concerned. As the train proceeds on its way and occupies track circuits in sequence, the train description displayed on the control panel steps forward from berth to berth accordingly. There is one exception to this in older power signalboxes: if the train passes a signal at Danger the track-circuit indications on the control panel will step forward normally, but the train description remains in the berth on the approach side of the signal concerned; the train description itself does not pass a signal at Danger. This provides important evidence in cases whereby a signal is wrongly passed at Danger and the aspect displayed by the signal is disputed by the driver.

In most signalboxes, the control panel is arranged almost vertically, and combines both the controls and the indications. The signaller walks to and fro to reach the various controls on that section of the panel under his jurisdiction. In some of the larger and busier signalboxes, such as

those at London Bridge and Victoria, the controls are removed from the panel and provided on a separate console at which the signaller sits. This is more expensive but enables the signaller to have a wider overview of the panel, and may lead to the improved regulation of trains in dense and complex traffic conditions.

The control panels contain other equipment besides the geographical display, such as:

1. Individual point switches, for movements of the points in special circumstances
2. Indicators, showing which way the points are lying. The two positions are known as *normal* and *reverse*. There is a third indication, known as *out of correspondence*, which is illuminated when the points have failed to move across correctly from one position to the other, or when they have been damaged in an accident. Signals will not clear if points are showing 'out of correspondence'.
3. Telephones, giving communication at each signal with drivers and anyone else who may need to speak to the signaller, such as track workers and signal technicians. When the telephone is used, the number of the signal at which the telephone is located is

displayed on the panel to help the signaller to identify the origin of the call. The rules also require the caller to identify himself and say where he is standing. Communication can often only be established from the signal to the signalbox; the signaller may not be able to ring the telephone instrument at the signal. He should normally not need to do so, and it reduces the cost of the equipment.

4. Telephones, giving communication to stations, offices etc, through the normal railway telephone network
5. Radio equipment at some signalboxes, giving communication with drivers (and now found extensively over the network)
6. Level-crossing indications and controls
7. Hot-axlebox warning equipment (see Chapter 29)
8. 'Train ready to start' (TRS) indications. At larger stations, where trains may be detained for reasons not apparent to the signaller, it may be advantageous for the setting of the route to be delayed until the train is ready to depart, thus allowing the route to be used by other trains. When the train is ready to depart, the signaller is informed by the operation of a plunger on the platform by the supervisor, which causes a yellow light to flash on the control panel at the end of the platform concerned.
9. Releases to ground frames, shunt frames, level-crossing boxes etc
10. Emergency replacement buttons and indications, for automatic and semi-automatic signals
11. Automatic working of controlled signals. The signaller can convert a controlled signal to automatic operation by pressing an 'A' button sited next to the signal on his panel, after the route has been set. The 'A' button then shows a white light. Automatic operation can be cancelled at any time merely by pulling out the 'A' button, but doing this does not cancel the route.

In most recent signalboxes, known as *signalling-control centres* or *Integrated Electronic Control Centres* (IECCs), the signaller's control panel has been replaced by visual-display units (VDUs) and tracker-ball/keyboard operation. The whole of the track layout, together with all the indications, is not permanently displayed, but the signaller calls up (*i.e.* displays) on his screens the particular areas or indications that he requires.

The screens are capable of displaying either an overview covering a relatively large area but omitting some detail, or a smaller area including the detail. The principles of operation remain the same — in order to set a route, the signaller, by using the tracker-ball, moves the cursor on his VDU screen to the signal at the entrance to the route he wishes to set, then enters his command by depressing a button. He then moves the cursor to the exit signal of the route and activates the setting of the route. Alternatively the signaller can set the route by the use of the keyboard, entering the numbers of the entrance and exit signals.

VDU equipment is cheaper, and requires far less space, than conventional control panels; consequently the operating room can be smaller. Coupled with the technical change from relay interlocking to computer-based interlocking, the whole signalbox structure can be much smaller.

A predictable and repetitive train service lends itself readily to the use of computer-controlled automatic route-setting equipment. Routes are set by the computer as programmed, including decisions on priorities at junctions, and alterations in the case of late running.

Event recorders are installed in modern signalboxes and remote interlockings, to record such things as signal aspect changes and the lie of points. This information is especially useful to incident investigators.

Above: A ground frame at Derby. The levers are released from the Signalling Centre. *Author*

Signalling a passenger train into an occupied platform (permissive working)

When the signaller wishes to set up a route for a passenger train from a controlled signal into an occupied permissive platform line, he will set the route in the normal way, but the main signal aspect remains at red, owing to the occupation of a track circuit in the route ahead. In such circumstances, authority for the driver to proceed is given by the exhibition of two white lights inclined at 45° in the associated position-light signal. These are the only circumstances in which the driver of a passenger train may proceed on the authority of a position-light signal. In the case of a through platform line at a station where the train is not booked to call, the signaller must advise the driver of the circumstances before clearing the signal.

Permissive working of this nature can be avoided in new installations by, for example, the provision of mid-platform signals on through platforms of sufficient length.

Lamp failures in colour-light running signals (lamp proving)

Where colour-light signals are fitted with filament bulbs rather than LEDs each bulb has both a main filament and an auxiliary filament. Any failure of a main filament causes an indication of the fact to be given in the signalbox. If a lamp that should be illuminated fails completely, the next main running signal on the approach side will be maintained at red, in order to ensure safety.

Numbering of colour-light signals

Each signal post carries a plate bearing the signal identity, comprising one or two prefix letters (identifying the controlling signalbox) followed by a number unique to that prefix. Odd numbers are used for the down direction, with the numbers ascending in the direction of the traffic flow. Even numbers are used for the up direction,

descending in the direction of the traffic flow. Automatic signals are identified as such to the driver by a horizontal black band on the identity plate. Semi-automatic signals carry the word 'SEMI' on the plate, above the horizontal band. Older installations may vary from the above.

Remote-control standby arrangements

Standby arrangements, known as *override facilities*, are provided at the older power signalboxes to deal with any failure of the cable between the signalbox and remote interlockings. These standby arrangements enable train movements to continue, but line capacity is reduced. In newer installations the control link (known as *time-division multiplex* or TDM) is duplicated to avoid the provision of expensive override facilities and to reduce the disruption of train services.

Signals from sidings onto running lines

A main signal (rather than a position-light ground signal) is provided at the exit from sidings where there are regular right-away movements and the next signal ahead is not visible from the siding exit (or is a long distance ahead).

Colour-light signals not in use

When main or position-light aspects are not in use they are covered over. A large 'X' may also be exhibited over the cover of main aspects.

Delayed-yellow operation

Where it is operationally desirable to allow a passenger train to approach a signal where the full overlap is not available (*i.e.* a *restricted overlap*), the next signal in rear is held at red until the train is close to it, after which it will clear to yellow. This is to ensure that the speed of the train is suitably reduced, and is a colour-light version of the Absolute Block 'section clear but station or junction blocked' warning arrangement.

(1) a controlled signal   (2) an automatic signal and   (3) a semi-automatic signal

Above: Signal-plates showing

This chapter describes what happens in the case of various types of failure and emergency when they occur in colour-light areas.

Complete failure of signalling apparatus

In the event of a complete failure of the signalling equipment affecting several signals along a substantial length of route, a substitute system of *temporary block working* is introduced. Handsignallers are appointed, and there must be communication between them and the signaller. Handsignallers are posted at signals at strategic locations, and *temporary block working* is introduced between them, under the instructions of the signaller. The handsignaller completes a temporary block working ticket and gives it to the driver. The ticket may authorise the driver to pass two or more consecutive signals.

If there is no telephone communication, competent people must be posted to strategic locations, which become in effect temporary block posts. Trains are worked in accordance with a time interval system, the driver being told where the next emergency block post is.

There are detailed instructions in Rule Book Modules S5, 'Passing a signal at danger', and T8, 'Handsignalling duties'. These and other Rule Book modules can be accessed either via the Rail Safety and Standards Board website or the Railway Group Standards website.

Track-circuit irregularities

Track circuits are so designed that when they fail to operate correctly they fail safe, *i.e.* they switch protecting signals to Danger and lock points etc. Any failure that did not initiate such safeguards would be very serious; such failures (fortunately rare) are known as *wrong-side failures*.

A signaller becomes aware of such an irregularity, commonly but incorrectly called a track-circuit failure, when the red track-circuit lights are illuminated on the panel or displayed on a VDU when there is no train on that section of the line, or when the red lights fail to go out after a train has passed and the following track circuit has cleared. The most likely cause is a failure of equipment, but the signaller must not assume that that is the cause. On the contrary, he must assume that the line may be obstructed and must find out whether it is or not. In the meantime trains will be at a standstill because the protecting signal will be at red.

Unless the signaller can establish that the line is clear (*e.g.* by telephoning a station supervisor, if the track circuit concerned is near the station), he must arrange for the line to be examined. It is usually most convenient to do this by using a train, and the driver must be informed of the circumstances, instructed to proceed cautiously over the affected portion of line prepared to stop short of any obstruction, and to report his findings. He need not be accompanied specially.

Any class of train may be used, irrespective of the weather, except that complications arise when any part of the track circuit is within a tunnel. A train may still be used for examination purposes, but the driver of the first train over the affected line is instructed to proceed with extreme caution, and

Right: A track circuit operating clip for use in an emergency. It short-circuits the electrical circuit and causes the indicator in the signalbox to show 'Occupied'. *Ian Allan Library*

not to exceed 10mph (16km/h) on the portion of line containing the track circuit concerned; however, if this train is used before the line has been examined by a train on the unaffected line, a passenger train must not be used on the affected line unless it can be established that the tunnel is clear, if necessary by a competent person walking through.

If it is established that there is no obstruction causing the track circuit to show occupied, it must be considered as having failed, and following trains may be allowed to proceed, each driver being authorised to pass the protecting signal at Danger. While the failure exists, however, the signaller has no way of knowing whether the piece of line concerned is clear or not; therefore he must take one of two possible precautions:

1. Appoint someone suitable to stand at the track circuit to report whether it is clear after each train has passed
2. Carefully watch, on his panel or VDU, the passage of each train and see that it occupies and clears the track circuit ahead of the signal beyond the failed track circuit. Drivers must be instructed to proceed cautiously, because the signaller cannot be 100% sure that the line is clear.

Axle-counter failures

Axle counters are subject to special arrangements to ensure that after the failure has been rectified, the line ahead is safe for trains to run on. Axle counters are returned to service by a dual process of reset and restoration, following which the section of line concerned must be examined as described below.

Examination of the line

If there is reason to believe, owing to some emergency or other, that the line may be blocked or unsafe to use, a train may be allowed to enter the section on any line in the right direction to examine the line. The term 'examination of line' is not confined solely to the track itself but includes anything out of the ordinary that may endanger a train. It also includes all lines in the section concerned, not just the line that the train is running on. The precise Rule Book wording, 'examine the line to see if it is clear' really means 'look out for any source of danger on any line'. Certain provisos have to be observed:

1. A passenger train must not be used during fog or falling snow (in case a train should

run into an obstruction in poor visibility).
2. A passenger train must not be allowed to enter a tunnel unless it is known that the area to be examined is not in the tunnel, or it has been established that the tunnel is clear (a competent person can walk through it to do this).
3. The driver must be accompanied by the guard or other competent person in the following circumstances: (i) during fog or falling snow; (ii) during darkness; (iii) through a tunnel (unless it is adequately illuminated).

The purpose of having the driver accompanied is to provide an extra pair of eyes. 'Competent' means having sufficient railway experience to be able to recognise a potential hazard.

The driver of the examining train must be told about what is going on and instructed to proceed cautiously, ready to stop at any moment if he sees an obstruction or any other source of danger ahead. After the examining train has entered the affected section of line, no other train may enter the same section on the same or an adjacent line until the signaller has received a report stating which lines are safe for trains to run on.

Report of a suspected track defect

From time to time, drivers feel a bump or jolt that is more severe than the usual bumps that are part and parcel of most journeys. They must then stop at the first available signal and report the facts to the signaller so that following trains can be stopped, in case a dangerous defect has developed in the track, or it is obstructed in some way. It is quite possible that by the time the signaller has received the report, a following train may also have passed over the bump, but it will probably be running under caution signals and slowing down.

The signaller must then arrange for the line to be examined, as described above. If no reason for the bump can be found, normal working may be resumed on other lines, but on the affected line drivers must be stopped and told about what has happened and instructed to proceed cautiously. This procedure must be continued for each following train until the affected line has been examined and confirmed to be safe by a person in charge of work on railway infrastructure. It is important that drivers reporting a bump should be as precise as possible regarding its location, and at all costs avoid giving a misleading location. It is equally important that the track-maintenance staff be sure that any defect they find is the one reported by the driver.

Suspected damage to track or structures

A train must not pass over a portion of line affected by subsidence or by suspected damage to a structure above or beneath the railway unless the signaller has been assured that it is safe for the train to do so, travelling at reduced speed if necessary.

If a railway bridge over a road has been hit by a road vehicle (an occurrence known as *bridge-bashing*), trains must be stopped until the bridge has been examined. If a Bridge Examining Engineer is not immediately available, the bridge may be examined by a Bridge Strike Nominee. If the damage is only superficial, the Bridge Strike Nominee may allow trains to pass over the bridge at 5mph (8km/h) in the case of a rail-over-road bridge, or at up to 20mph (32km/h) where the bridge is over the railway, pending an examination by a Bridge Examining Engineer. Rule Book Module TS1 'General signalling regulations' gives detailed guidance on these issues.

Broken rails in continuous welded track

A broken rail may be detected in a number of ways:

1. If there is a gap between the two broken ends, any track-circuit current flowing through the rail is interrupted, causing the track-circuit indication on the signalbox panel to show 'occupied', and switching the signal in rear (*i.e.* on the approach side) to Danger.

2. It may be noticed by the track patroller on his regular routine inspection or by some other member of staff.

3. A driver passing over the spot may feel an unusual bump, which he will stop and report, prompting an examination of the track.

The question then arises whether trains may be allowed to pass over the break. If a person competent in track examination is not immediately available a person who has been certified as competent in the instructions in Section V of the Rule Book may authorise trains to proceed over a broken or distorted rail at 5mph (8km/h) provided that certain conditions are met, including:

1. The rail is in plain line
2. The rail is not in a tunnel
3. The adjacent sleepers and fastenings are in good condition
4. The detailed conditions listed in the Rule Book concerning the nature of the break or damage are applied.

The rail must be carefully examined before each train passes over it, to ensure that it is safe to do so. While a train is passing over the break, no train may be allowed to pass over an adjoining line (a safety precaution in case the train passing over the break becomes derailed).

PART 3

Chapter 11   The Absolute Block system of signalling

The Absolute Block system is the traditional way of signalling trains, which was developed during the 19th century and refined during the first half of the 20th century. It is now largely superseded on main lines by the track-circuit block system, though there are still several hundreds of the familiar signalboxes on secondary lines.

The Absolute Block system might be summed up in the principle, set out in the regulations for many, many years, that 'not more than one train shall be in a block section on the same line at the same time'. So what is a block section? It is that piece of line between the last signal passed by a train at one signalbox and the first stop signal at the next signalbox.

The last signal passed by a train at a signalbox controls the entrance to a block section and is known as a *section signal* (or sometimes as the *most advanced signal*). The first stop signal at a signalbox is known as the *home signal*. At some signalboxes there may be more than one home signal, known variously as *outer and inner home

signals*, or *home Nos 1 and 2 signals*. In such cases the first one to be encountered by a train is known as the *outermost home signal* (or alternatively the *outermost stop signal*). The section of line between the outermost stop signal and the most advanced signal worked from the same signalbox is known as *station limits*. Station limits separate the block sections from each other.

In railway parlance, the terms *advanced* and *rear*, first introduced in Chapter 3, may be

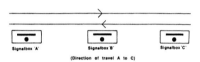

Above: An illustration of the meaning of the terms 'rear section' and 'advance section'. For a train travelling from A to C the rear section for the signaller at B is A-B, and the advance section is B-C

Above: A newly painted traditional signalbox at Oakham. *D. C. Hall*

confusing, and are best illustrated in the diagram below. So far as signalbox B is concerned, for a train travelling from A to C the *rear section* is A-B and the *advance section* is B-C.

In order to send train-signalling messages from one signalbox to the next a bell system is used, with the messages being described by the number and pattern of beats on the bell. Instruments, known as *block indicators*, are provided in each signalbox for each section and each direction. Slave instruments are provided in the next signalbox. In the controlling signalbox, the standard block indicator can be moved to one of three positions — 'Normal' (line blocked), 'Line clear' and 'Train on line'. When there is no train in the area the line is considered blocked, which might be considered a misnomer. What it means is that the line is not at that moment being used by a train, therefore it is temporarily out of use and must not be considered to be clear until the signaller says that it is. It is also a means of compelling the signaller at the box in rear to ask for permission to send a train through the section. At some signalboxes there are older block instruments of different types, which date back to the old pre-1923 companies.

If we consider our three signalboxes A, B and C again, the method of passing a train along the line is as follows.

When the signaller at box A wishes to arrange for a train to proceed from A to B, he calls the attention of the signaller at box B by sending one beat on the bell (known as the *block bell*). B responds with one beat. A then sends the appropriate bell signal for the type of train (*e.g.* four beats for an express passenger train). If B is satisfied that there is no train in the section A-B and that the block indicator for that section is at the 'Normal' position (line blocked), he may accept the train by repeating the four beats bell signal and moving his block indicator to 'Line clear'. The slave indicator in box A also moves to 'Line clear' as a reminder to the signaller there, and he may then clear his signals for the train. In most signalboxes there is an electrical lock on the most advanced signal that prevents the signal from being cleared until the block indicator shows 'Line clear'. Furthermore, as an additional precaution, the signal can only be cleared once for each 'Line clear'.

When the train passes A, the signaller there must send the 'Train entering section' signal to B,

Above: Traditional block instruments still in use at Stockport No 2 signalbox, working to Heaton Norris Junction signalbox and Stockport No 1 signalbox. *D. C. Hall*

who must repeat it back and move his block indicator to 'Train on line'. B must then seek acceptance of the train from the signaller at C and clear his own signals.

When the train passes B, the signaller sends the 'Train entering section' signal to C, and when the train, complete with its tail lamp (see below), has passed the clearing point at B (normally ¼ mile past the outermost stop signal at B), the signaller at B calls the attention of A (one beat) and, having obtained it (one beat repeated back), sends the 'Train out of section' signal (two beats, pause, one beat) and moves the block indicator to the 'normal' position (line blocked). A can now offer (*i.e.* seek acceptance of) another train to B.

To avoid the danger that might arise if a signaller were mistakenly to give the 'Train out of section' signal while the train was still in the rear section, special equipment is provided at some signalboxes that locks the block indicator at 'Train on line' until the train is proved to have passed through the section by the occupation of a track circuit, or the actuation of a treadle, at the home signal. A release mechanism is provided for use in case of equipment failure or when a train that has been signalled forward is cancelled. Three different release systems are in use:

1. The 'Welwyn control' system. Before the block indicator can be released a small wheel has to be rotated about a hundred times, which gives the signaller time for second thoughts and allows a train that is still in the rear section more time to reach the home signal and safety. It has proved a very effective system since it was first introduced after an accident at Welwyn Garden City in 1935, and is now the standard system.
2. Sykes 'lock and block'. This linked the block instruments mechanically with the signal levers, compelling the signalman to restore these levers after the arrival of each train, before a second 'Line clear' release could be given. The release takes the form of a key, but its misuse has caused a number of accidents. An additional safeguard was a rail-mounted electric treadle at the home signal, which prevented a second 'Line clear' release from being given until the first train had arrived and operated the treadle. The Sykes system was introduced in the 19th century and was at one time in widespread use, especially on the former Southern Railway, but it has been replaced in most cases by modern power signalling.
3. Midland Railway 'rotary block'. The block instrument can only be moved in rotation from the 'Normal' position, through 'Line clear', to 'Train on line' and back to 'Normal'. To cancel a 'Line clear' the two signallers have to agree and simultaneously press a cancelling button. To release the block indicator from 'Train on line' the signaller has to press a button to which access can be gained only by breaking a glass cover. The signaller must then send a report to his supervisor and call for the signalling-maintenance staff to replace the glass cover.

Every train carries at the rear of the last vehicle either a detachable tail lamp or a built-in tail lamp displaying a red light, to prove to the signaller that it is complete and that that no part of it has been accidentally left in the rear section. Signallers must carefully observe the tail lamp before sending the 'Train out of section' signal.

Where sections are short, the signaller may be authorised to send the 'Is line clear?' signal to the box in advance as soon as he has accepted the train from the box in rear. This avoids drivers' seeing the signals before they have been cleared, which would cause delay.

Where a signaller needs to know about the approach of a train before he receives the 'Train entering section' signal, for example to give him time to close level crossing gates or barriers across the road, the signaller in rear may be authorised to send the 'Train approaching' signal (1–2–1) when the train passes a predetermined point (usually the previous signalbox).

The bell codes used to signal trains in the Absolute Block system are as follows:

	Number of beats
Call attention	1
Is line clear?	
Class 0 train	2–3
Class 1 train	4
Class 2 train	3–1
Class 3 train	1–3–1
Class 4 train	3–1–1
Class 5 train	2–2–1
Class 6 train	5
Class 7 train	4–1
Class 8 train	3–2
Class 9 train	1–4
Class 9 train (*empty coaching stock*)	1–4–1
Train requiring to stop in section	2–2–3

Details of the train classes are as follows:

0 Light engine(s)
1 Express passenger train
  Nominated postal or parcels train
  Breakdown or overhead-line-equipment train going to clear the line or returning therefrom (1Z99)
  Traction unit going to assist a disabled train (1Z99)
  Snowplough going to clear the line (1Z99)
2 Ordinary passenger train
  Breakdown or overhead-line-equipment train not going to clear the line (2Z99)
  Officer's special train (2Z01)
3 Freight train capable of running at more than 75mph
  Parcels train
  Empty coaching stock (where specially authorised)
4 Freight train permitted to run at up to 75mph
5 Empty coaching stock
6 Freight train permitted to run at up to 60mph
7 Freight train permitted to run at up to 45mph
8 Freight train permitted or timed to run at 35mph or less
9 Class 373 train (Eurostar)

Other bell signals are:

	Number of beats
Train entering section	2
Train approaching	1–2–1
Cancelling	3–5
Train incorrectly described	5–3
Restricted acceptance	3–5–5
Line now clear in accordance with Regulation 3, clause 3.4, for the train to approach	3–3–5
Train out of section } Obstruction removed }	2–1
Locomotive assisting in rear of train	2–2
Obstruction danger	6
Train an unusually long time in section	6–2
Stop and examine train	7
Train passed without tail lamp	9 to box in advance 4–5 to box in rear
Train or vehicles running away in wrong direction	2–5–5
Train or vehicles running away in right direction	4–5–5

There are a number of other bell signals with which we need not concern ourselves.

The 'Call attention' signal (one beat) must be sent and acknowledged before any other bell signal is sent, except for the following:

	Number of beats
Train entering section	2
Train approaching	1–2–1
Restricted acceptance	3–5–5
Locomotive assisting in rear of train	2–2
Obstruction danger	6
Police assistance urgently required	1–1–6
Answer telephone	1–1
Distant signal defective	8–2
Home signal defective	2–8

Generally speaking, bell signals are acknowledged by repetition and must not be considered as correctly understood until correctly repeated. If the 'Is line clear?' signal is not acknowledged (*i.e.* if the request for acceptance is refused) it must be sent again at short intervals. In railway parlance, trains are 'offered' and either accepted or refused.

The bell signal 'Answer telephone' is only to be used for the block telephone, which is a special circuit connecting only the two signalboxes.

Train regulation
Trains generally take precedence according to classification.

Semaphore signals are of four types:

1. Distant signals
2. Stop signals
3. Subsidiary signals
4. Shunting signals

Distant and stop signals

Distant and stop signals are used to control normal train movements. A distant signal takes the form of a rectangular yellow arm with a fishtail end and a black chevron. A stop signal has a red rectangular arm and a white vertical stripe. The backs of the signal arms are white, with a black chevron or bar. The indications to drivers are as follows.

Distant signals

When the arm is horizontal the driver must get ready to stop at the next stop signal. When the arm is pivoted upwards or downwards through approximately 45° it means that all stop signals for the line concerned that are worked from the same signalbox are clear. At night the 'caution' indication is given by a yellow light. The 'clear' indication is given by a green light.

Stop signals

When the arm is horizontal (red light at night), it means Stop. When the arm is pivoted up or down through approximately 45° (green light at night), it means Proceed.

Subsidiary signals

A subsidiary signal is placed below the main arm of a stop signal and takes the form of a small red arm (or a white arm with horizontal red stripes). Subsidiary signals are of two types, called *calling-on signals* and *shunt ahead signals*, distinguished by the letter 'C' or 'S'. They have no meaning when the arm is horizontal (although they may show a red or white light), but when the arm is pivoted up or down by approximately 45° they mean:

1. Calling-on signals — Proceed cautiously towards the next stop signal (or buffer stops). There may be a train on the line ahead, so be ready to stop short of it.
2. Shunt-ahead signals — Proceed for shunting purposes only.

Above: A fine array of semaphore signals at the west end of Southampton Central station, photographed in 1981. Each group of three signals refers to one route with two routes diverging from it. *C. J. Tuffs*

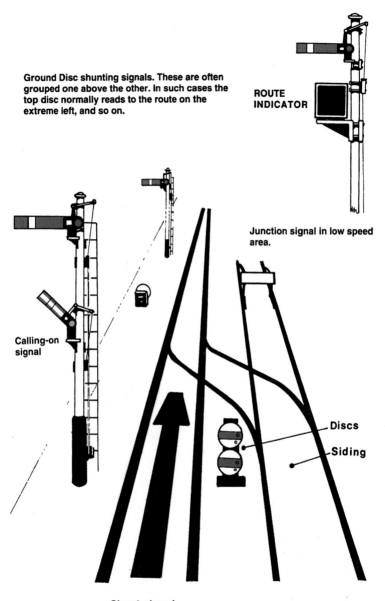

Ground Disc shunting signals. These are often grouped one above the other. In such cases the top disc normally reads to the route on the extreme left, and so on.

ROUTE INDICATOR

Junction signal in low speed area.

Calling-on signal

Discs

Siding

Shunt ahead

Above: Subsidiary and shunting signals. The top disc reads to the route to the left.

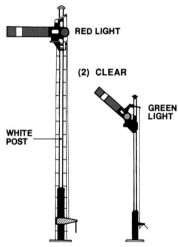

(1) CAUTION

YELLOW
LIGHT

(2) CLEAR

GREEN
LIGHT

Above: A distant signal showing
(1) Caution and
(2) Clear.

(1) STOP - DANGER

RED LIGHT

(2) CLEAR

GREEN
LIGHT

WHITE
POST

STOP   PROCEED

Above: A Stop signal showing
(1) Danger — Stop, and
(2) Clear — Proceed.

In each case the main stop signal arm will remain at Danger.

Shunting signals
Shunting signals are usually fixed near the ground and take the form of a white disc or small arm. The disc has a red stripe, which is horizontal in the normal (Stop) position. The small arm is also horizontal for Stop, and a red or white light is displayed at night. The Proceed indication is given by the disc being rotated or the arm being pivoted up or down through approximately 45°, with a green light at night. In this case, 'Proceed' applies only as far as the line is clear.

A few shunting signals have a black disc with a yellow stripe, or a yellow arm, especially where shunting movements pass to and fro over a set of points normally lying in a particular direction. The signal may be ignored in such circumstances, but if a movement is to be made over the points when they have been turned to the other direction, the signal must be obeyed.

Above: An unusual four-disc shunting signal at Forder's Siding on the East Coast main line, which has only recently been taken out of use. *D. C. Hall*

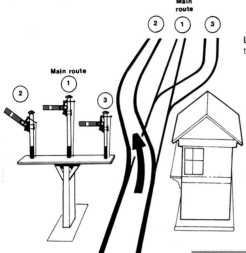

Main route

2 1 3

Left: A junction signal, with a taller post for the main route

Main route

1

2 3

Below: Junction signals at Worcester Shrub Hill station. The distant signals are permanently fixed at Caution. *D. C. Hall*

Junction stop signals (geographic or otherwise)

The positioning and stepping of signals is as follows (see diagram opposite? above? below?):

Signal 1 applies to the straight route.
Signal 2 applies to the diverging route to the left.
Signal 3 applies to the diverging route to the right.

The vertical arrangement is normally used only for shunting signals.

Where speeds are low, for example in station areas, only one signal is provided in some cases, and the route is indicated by a figure or letter near to the signal arm.

Banner repeating signals

As in colour-light areas, banner repeaters are provided on the approach to signals to assist the driver in those cases where the sighting of the main signal is restricted, for example by curvature of the line, or by buildings, tunnels etc. They are identical to those used in colour-light areas (see Chapter 5) except that the semaphore arm (or its representation by fibre optics or LEDs) has a square end for a stop signal and a fishtail end for a distant signal. The banner indication is always in the same position (horizontal or turned through 45°) as the main signal arm.

The following drawings show the typical arrangement of signals at a station and a junction.

At a station
The names of the signals are as follows.

1. Up Distant
    Cannot be cleared until 2 and 3 have been cleared.
2. Up Home (stop)
    Cannot be cleared if 3 is at Clear. It is also the outermost stop signal.
3. Up Starting (stop)
    Cannot normally be cleared unless the block indicator at 'Z' is at the 'line clear' position. This signal may also be referred to in some circumstances as the Platform Starting signal. It may also be referred to as the Up Section signal, because it allows access to the up section.
4. Down Distant
    Cannot be cleared until 5, 6 and 7 have been cleared.
5. Down Home No 1 (stop)
    Cannot be cleared if 6 or 7 are at Clear. It is also the outermost stop signal.
6. Down Home No 2 (stop)
    Cannot be cleared if 7 is at Clear. It may also be referred to as the Platform Starting signal in some circumstances.
7. Down Starting (stop)
    Cannot normally be cleared unless the block indicator at 'Y' is at the 'line clear' position. It may also be referred to as the Down Section signal.

8. Calling-on
    Allows a second train to enter the platform (*e.g.* for connecting purposes). The signal must not be cleared until the train has stopped or nearly stopped at it, in order to ensure that the train proceeds into the station at a very low speed.
9. Shunting
    Setting back down main to up main.
10. Shunting
    Setting back down main to sidings.
11. Shunting
    Setting back up main to down main.
12. Shunting
    Sidings to down main.

The points and signals are interlocked so that the signals cannot be cleared until the points are in the corresponding position.

At a junction
The names of the signals are as follows:

1. Up Distant
    Can only be cleared for the straight route to 'Z'. This ensures that the driver reduces speed for the junction turnout if proceeding to 'Y'. Occasionally an arm may be provided for each route.
2. Up Home to 'Y'
3. Up Home to 'Z'
4. Up Starting to 'Y'
5. Down Distant from 'Y'
6. Down Outer Home from 'Y'
    This is an additional signal, ¼ mile from No 7, which allows the signaller to accept a train

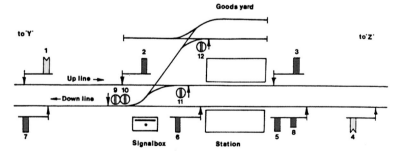

Above: Typical arrangement of signals at a station.

Below: Typical arrangement of signals at a junction.

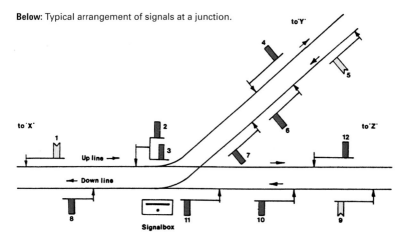

from 'Y' while the signals have been cleared for a train to or from 'Z'.

7. Down Inner Home from 'Y'
8. Down Starting
9. Down Distant from 'Z'
10. Down Outer Home from 'Z'
    This is an additional signal, ¼ mile from No 11, which allows the signaller to accept a train from 'Z' whilst the signals have been cleared for a train from 'Y'.
11. Down Inner Home from 'Z'
12. Up Starting to 'Z'

The sequential locking of signals, and the interlocking of points and signals, are as shown above under the heading 'At a station'.

The starting signals are sometimes referred to as section signals.

Train detection by track circuit or axle counter

Track circuits (or axle counters in some cases) are provided only where traffic and other considerations justify it. A typical arrangement, based on the station drawing, would be:

Station limits (between signals 2 and 3 on the up line, 5 and 7 on the down line) are fully track-circuited, but divided into several separate sections. The track circuits, when occupied, have the following effects.

Track circuits A and D

These are known as *berth track circuits*. They ensure that a train is safely protected when standing at the home signal, by electrically locking the block indicator at 'train on line'. This in turn ensures that the signallers at 'Y' and 'Z'

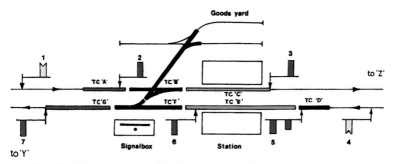

Above: Typical arrangements of track circuits at a station.

49

cannot clear their starting signals to allow another train to approach. Furthermore, the block indicator for the rear section cannot be released until the train has occupied and cleared these track circuits; this ensures that the signaller cannot inadvertently release the block indicator for the rear section while there is still a train in it.

Track circuit B
Locks signal 2 at Danger and locks the points.

Track circuit C
Locks signal 2 at Danger.

Track circuit E
Locks signal 5 at Danger.

Track circuit F
Locks signal 6 at Danger and locks the points.

Track circuit G
Locks signal 6 at Danger.

One of the main features of such track circuits is that they guard against the possibly disastrous consequences of the signaller forgetting about a train or locomotive standing within his station limits. They also prevent points from being moved under a train.

Track circuits A and D also perform another function. The block indicators at 'Y' and 'Z' electrically lock at Danger signals 2 and 5, the signals being released either when the block indicator is moved to 'Line clear' or when a train occupies those track circuits. This ensures that signals 2 and 5 cannot be cleared until the train is slowing down ready to stop at the signal, unless it has already been accepted by 'Y' or 'Z'. Without such an arrangement, a driver might see the home signal at Clear some distance away and overlook the starting signal at Danger, causing the train to enter the section ahead without having been accepted by the signaller.

It can be seen that berth track circuits A and D perform several vital safety functions, but there is yet another. If a train should occupy a berth track circuit when, owing to some misunderstanding between the signallers, it had been allowed to enter the rear section without the block instrument having been placed at 'Train on line', the block instrument would immediately move to 'Train on line' as a safety measure. When a train first occupies a berth track circuit a buzzer (known as an *annunciator*) will sound if the

home signal is at Danger, to draw the signaller's attention to the fact and inform him that he may now clear the signal if conditions ahead allow (and always provided that the signaller is satisfied that the speed of the train has been suitably reduced).

Other safety controls
Three other safety controls must be mentioned:
1. Sequential locking
2. Home normal contact
3. Distant arm proving

Sequential locking
The signal levers are interlocked and must be pulled off (*i.e.* cleared) in a predetermined order. Referring to the station drawing, the order would be:

Up line
1. Home signal (No 2)
2. Starting signal (No 3)
3. Distant signal (No 1)

Down line
1. Home No 1 signal (No 5)
2. Home No 2 signal (No 6)
3. Starting signal (No 7)
4. Distant signal (No 4)

The distant signal must be replaced first, but the stop signals can be replaced in any order.

Home normal contact
There is electrical locking between the home signal lever and the block indicator for the rear section, which ensures that the block indicator cannot be moved to the 'Line clear' position unless the home signal lever is back in the frame in the normal position, with the signal at Danger. It compels the signaller to restore all signals to Danger after the passage of each train.

Distant arm proving
The position of the distant signal arm (*i.e.* caution or clear) is indicated on an instrument in the signalbox and electrically interlocked with the block indicator in such a manner that the block indicator cannot be moved to the 'Line clear' position unless the distant signal arm is at Caution.

Use of colour-light signals in Absolute Block signalling
For many years it has been the practice to replace isolated semaphore distant signals with

a colour-light signal that can show a yellow or a green light. Colour-light signals show up more clearly in the dark, and no special precautions are necessary during fog or falling snow. The clearing point is 200 yards (180m)

Occasionally the home signal itself may be replaced by a colour-light signal, in which case it has three aspects — red, yellow and green. It shows a yellow aspect if the starting signal is at Danger, and the distant signal may be modified to show two yellow lights. This arrangement only applies where certain distance criteria are met.

Finally, the starting signal may be replaced by a colour-light signal, in which case it has two aspects — red and green.

The use of colour-light signals in this way can be especially convenient where the sections are short, and the distant signals for one signalbox are mounted underneath the stop signals of the signalbox in rear, on the same post. Incidentally, in the latter case the distant and stop signal arms are mechanically 'slotted' together (*i.e.* interlocked), so that the distant signal cannot show Clear when the stop signal is at Danger.

Safety at points

Measures must be taken to ensure that *facing points* are lying in the correct position for the safety of an approaching train. (Facing points are those that can change the direction of a train approaching them. For trains coming the other way they are known as *trailing points*.) This is achieved in a number of ways:

1. Interlocking between the levers operating the points and signals, so that a wrong signal cannot be cleared

2. Detection on site between the point blades and the signal. A slotted bar runs at right angles from each point blade to a detector. When the points are fitting correctly, and only then, another slotted bar in the wire operating the signal is able to slide through at a right angle in the detector. This ensures that the points are fitting correctly and that only the correct signal can be cleared. (See drawing.)

3. To guard against danger in the event of the signaller's inadvertently replacing the signal to Danger and moving the points as the train is about to pass over them, or is actually doing so, a long pivoted bar is fixed to the inside of one of the rails immediately preceding the point. This bar is operated by a lever in the signalbox, and when the lever is moved, the bar swings up to rail level, an operation that is physically impossible when the flange of a wheel is pressing down on the bar. In many cases the bar has been replaced by a track circuit which, when occupied, locks the lever which locks the points.

4. The points are physically secured by a bolt or plunger that passes through a hole in a bar connecting the two point blades. The bolt is worked by a lever in the signalbox, which is interlocked with the signal levers. The bolt cannot be withdrawn when the signal is at Clear, nor can the signal be cleared unless the bolt is detected as being through the hole in the bar connecting the two point blades (see above).

5. An automatic time release (known as a *back lock*) on signals protecting points

Simplified diagram showing the detection between signals and facing points. In practice there are generally three slides from the points — one from each blade and one from the facing point lock. All must be in their correct position for the signal slide to pass freely.

Above: Mechanical detector at facing points.

51

One other piece of apparatus must be mentioned — the *fouling bar*. When a train has passed through a facing point, the last vehicle has to proceed sufficiently far beyond the junction before a following train can pass safely through the junction to the other route. The precise spot to which the line beyond the facing points must be clear is known as the *fouling point*, and sometimes in station areas a spring-loaded bar, known as a *fouling bar* or *depression bar*, may be fixed to the inside of the rail up to the fouling point. The wheel flange of any vehicle standing on the depression bar presses it down and operates an electrical contact that locks the signals concerned. In calculating the required length of the depression bar, regard must be paid to the maximum possible overhang at the ends of vehicles and the distance between the inside wheelsets of bogies. The same effect can be obtained by the use of track circuits.

Note:

Not all the safety controls described in this chapter are provided in every signalbox. Their provision depends on the number and speed of trains, importance of the line etc.

Acceptance of trains

Under Absolute Block Regulation 3.4, a train may only be accepted by a signaller during clear weather when the following conditions are met:

1. The line is clear to the clearing point — 200 yards (180m) beyond the home signal if the distant signal is a colour-light signal and 440 yards (400m) if the distant signal is a semaphore. This is the safety margin known as the *overlap*.
2. All points between the home signal and the clearing point are correctly set and locked for the safety of the approaching train.
3. No conflicting movement has been authorised that will cross or foul the safety overlap.
4. No other train has been accepted whose acceptance required it to occupy any portion of that safety overlap; in other words, once the overlap has been 'promised' to a train, it cannot be promised to another at the same time.

In normal circumstances, after a train has been accepted, the line on which it will run must be kept clear until either the train has stopped at the home signal or has passed beyond any points that need to be used within the safety overlap, or its journey has been cancelled.

Acceptance in fog or falling snow

Certain additional conditions apply when a train is accepted in fog or falling snow:

1. If the distant signal is a colour-light and the home signal a semaphore, the overlap is 440 yards (400m).
2. If the distant signal is a semaphore, the advance section must also be clear, together with the overlap of the signalbox in advance. To enforce this, a train must not be accepted unless the 'Train out of section' bell signal has been received from the signalbox in advance and the block indicator for the advance section is in the 'normal' position (line blocked). This is known as *double-block working*.
3. If the home signal of the signalbox in advance is less than ½ mile (800m) from the signalbox in rear, then, as an additional

safety measure, the train must have been accepted by the signaller in advance before it can be accepted from the signaller in rear. To clarify this, let us take three signalboxes, A, B and C. Before B can accept a train from A he must have had it accepted by C.

4. If a train in Classes 1-6 has to be allowed to approach with the facing points set for an unbooked route that is speed-restricted, the signaller in rear must be told, and the train must be accepted in accordance with the 'restricted acceptance' Regulation 3.5 and not with the 'normal acceptance' Regulation 3.4.

The term *unbooked route* means a route not shown in the Working Timetable or in any supplement or in the Weekly Special Traffic Notice.

Restricted acceptance (Regulation 3.5)

This regulation is nowadays only used in accordance with the previous paragraph, or where single-line working is in operation, as shown in Regulation 9, or where engineering trains require to enter an *absolute possession* (T3) of the line where the detonator protection is within the clearing point.

The arrangements are described in the Absolute Block Regulations and apply where the line is clear only as far as the home signal but is not clear to the clearing point.

To accept a train under Regulation 3.5 the 'Is line clear?' signal must not be repeated back, but the 'Restricted acceptance' signal (3–5–5) must be sent instead. The signaller in rear will acknowledge this signal, after which the block indicator may be moved to 'Line clear'. If, before the train enters the section, the acceptance circumstances change to permit the train to be accepted under Regulation 3.4 in the normal way, the bell signal 'Line now clear in accordance with Regulation 3.4 for the train to approach' (3–3–5) must be sent.

If the section signal at the signalbox in rear cannot be cleared because it requires a 'Line clear' release that cannot be given because the block indicator is held at 'Train on line' by the occupation of a track circuit in the safety overlap, the driver, when being cautioned about the restricted acceptance, will be authorised to pass the section signal at Danger.

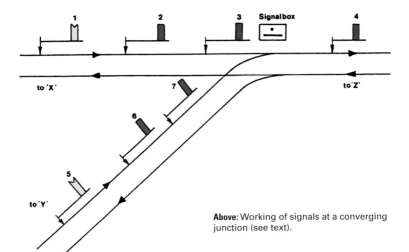

Above: Working of signals at a converging junction (see text).

Where engineering work is taking place within the clearing point a train may only be accepted under the Restricted Acceptance arrangements, and the driver must be told why.

Working of signals at converging junctions

Signals 2 and 6 are additional — or outer — home signals to allow trains to be accepted from X and Y simultaneously. They are at safety-overlap distance from signals 3 and 7, which become inner home signals. The outer home signal must not be cleared for a train from X when the signals have been cleared for a train from Y, but the train from X must be held at the outer home signal No 2, and *vice versa*.

'Train out of section' signal

The 'Train out of section' signal (2–1) must be sent and the block indicator placed to the normal position when the train has cleared the safety overlap. The signaller must ensure that there is a tail lamp on the last vehicle, as an assurance that no part of the train has been accidentally left in the section.

At signalboxes where the use of the Restricted Acceptance arrangement is in operation, the 2–1 bell signal should be sent as soon as the train has passed the home signal and while it is still in the safety overlap (provided the class of train is suitable, *i.e.* normally a freight train), but the block indicator must be maintained at 'Train on line' until the safety overlap is clear, whereupon it must be

moved to normal and one beat on the bell sent. Signallers normally use their discretion, and apply this procedure only if the train concerned is likely to occupy the safety overlap for more than the normal time.

If the train is shunted or diverted clear of the main line before it passes the signalbox and the signaller does not see the tail lamp, he must not send the 'Train out of section' signal until a member of the train crew has told him that the train is complete. Where such movements occur frequently, a telephone is normally provided to enable the train crew to speak to the signaller.

Working of signals when the train is not accepted by the signaller in advance

When a signaller offers a train to the signaller in advance but it is not accepted, he works his signals in a special way to reinforce the fact that the starting signal is at Danger. If the driver were to miss the starting signal and wrongly proceed into the next section a collision could result.

The signaller will keep all his signals at Danger until the train has almost stopped at the home signal, when he will clear them (slowly, in practice but not by rule) and allow the train forward. There is an exception to this rule where the stop signal in rear of the signal at Danger is a colour-light signal that can display a yellow aspect (special conditions apply).

Where there is a berth track circuit — usually 200 yards (180m) long — preceding the home signal, the signaller may clear the home signal as soon as the berth track circuit is occupied, provided he is satisfied that the train is slowing down to stop at the signal. This proviso is important.

The driver will draw slowly forward past the home signal, understanding that the next stop signal ahead may be at Danger. He keeps an eye on the signalbox to see whether the signaller is holding out a red flag or light, in which case the driver must stop there because the signaller needs to tell him something, which may be a cautionary instruction about the state of the line ahead. If the driver is stopped at the signalbox, he must not restart his train until the signaller has held out a green handsignal. If the driver has been instructed to pass a signal at Danger, a yellow handsignal is given instead of a green one.

Complications arise when the signaller cannot tell whether the starting signal is at Danger or not; it may be out of sight, and he may have no repeater. In such circumstances the train must be held at the signal in rear unless the driver can be told about it. During fog or falling snow a train must not be allowed to draw forward to a semaphore starting signal to await acceptance, in case the driver misses the signal altogether.

Replacing signals to Danger or Caution

The normal position of signals is Danger, or Caution in the case of distant signals. A distant signal must be replaced to Caution as soon as the signaller can tell that the train has passed the signal. A stop signal must be replaced to Danger as soon as the last vehicle of a train has passed it, except that where there are facing points beyond the signal, the signaller must wait until the last vehicle has passed those points before he replaces the signal to Danger.

Once the signaller has cleared his signals for a train he must not, except in emergency, replace them to Danger until the train has either passed or stopped at them. (There is an exception to this at junctions when the wrong priority has been given, but the signals may only be replaced to Danger if the train is sufficiently far away.)

If a signal is at Clear for a train to start (e.g. from a station) and the signaller requires to replace it to Danger before the train does start, he must make sure that the driver knows about it before the line ahead is obstructed or points are moved. This is to guard against the danger of the driver failing to check that the signal is still at Clear before he moves off.

After operating a lever the signaller must look to see (where he can) that the signal or points have moved correctly. If a repeater is provided, he must check such operation by reference to the repeater, where necessary. Wire adjusters are provided so that the signaller can tighten or slacken the wire operating the signal to cater for variations in temperature.

The signaller must watch the track-circuit indicators during the passage of trains, as far as practicable.

Working of signals at diverging junctions

If a train in Classes 1-6 is to be diverted from its booked route at a junction over which speed must be reduced, the junction signal must not be cleared until the train is close to it and, where practicable, the signaller is satisfied that its speed has been suitably reduced (not applicable if approach release arrangements are in operation). The term *booked route* means a route shown in the Working Timetable or in any supplement or in the Weekly Special Traffic Notice.

If the signaller cannot set the junction points until the train is close to the junction signal, he must as far as practicable ensure that it is safe to do so, having regard to the position and speed of the train.

Working in fog or falling snow

Instructions for working during fog or falling snow apply as soon as the *fog marking point*, normally a nominated signal, becomes obscured. If a fog marking point is not specified at a signalbox a distance of 200 yards (180m) will apply.

During severe frost the signaller must frequently work his signals, points etc, to prevent them from freezing up.

When a train has to be stopped by signals, for example because it has not been accepted by the signaller in advance, the signaller must, if practicable, place a detonator on the rail to warn a driver who may have failed to see the home signal at Danger. Detonators are small, round explosive devices which are fixed in an emergency to the top of the rail head by lead clips and are exploded by the wheels of a train passing over them, thus alerting the driver to any emergency. Detonator-placing machines ('detonator placers') are provided at most signalboxes, worked by a lever or handle in the signalbox itself, and can be used for this purpose. They are also available for use in any emergency, whether in clear or foggy weather.

Signalboxes are normally constructed with two storeys, the signaller being located on the upper floor to give him a better all-round view. The lower floor contains technical equipment. Before we enter the signalbox, however, we should observe the notice on the door which says 'Private' or 'No Admittance'. The signaller must not allow unauthorised people to enter.

The two main features of the interior of the signalbox are the frame containing all the levers and the shelf above it (known as the *block shelf*) carrying all the block instruments, bells, tappers, repeaters etc.

The levers are grouped for convenience, those most frequently used being towards the centre of the frame. Each lever has a locking catch or handle to secure its position in the frame. Levers are referred to as being *reversed* when pulled over and *replaced* when put back. They are painted in different colours for different functions, for example stop signal levers are red, distant signal levers are yellow, and points levers are black. Levers which are locked electrically by the block indicators have a white band. If the signal is a colour-light signal, or if the points are power-worked, the lever is cut short by six inches as a reminder to the signaller that little or no effort is needed to reverse the lever. Each lever is numbered and has a nameplate, which may bear the numbers of any levers that are interlocked with it.

When a signaller operates a lever, he must check that the signal or points concerned have gone to the correct position, either by direct observation, or by observing the appropriate indicator in the signalbox.

Above: Oakham signalbox, showing a rather jumbled array of signal arm and light repeaters and point repeaters. On the block shelf are the block instruments to and from the signalboxes on each side. Each block instrument contains, from top to bottom, a 'slave' indicator repeating the block indicator at one of the adjacent signalboxes, a block indicator operated by the signaller at Oakham, the switch for operating the block instrument, a bell for receiving messages, and a tapper key for sending messages. Also on the block shelf is an instrument associated with a nearby automatic half-barrier crossing. *D. C. Hall*

56

Above and below: Two views of the interior of Melton Station signalbox, showing (above) the lever frame, the block instruments and the various point and signal indicators, and (below) the illuminated track diagram, so called because lights indicate occupied track circuits. It covers the area under the control of the signaller, and shows the track layout and all the signals, points, level crossings and other features. *D. C. Hall*

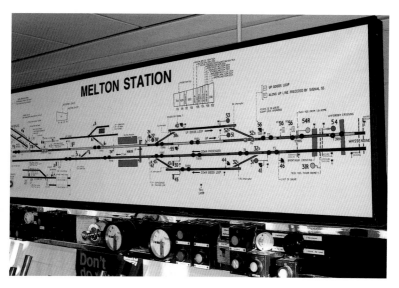

Above: Signals that have their backs to the signaller have a small aperture, known as a back light, in the back of the signal lamp casing, which indicates to the signaller during darkness whether the lamp is alight or not. The pivoted curved white plate swings in combination with the signal arm and obscures the back light when the arm is in the 'off' position, and indicates the position of the signal arm to the signaller. *Author*

The block shelf carries the electrically-operated instruments, such as:

1. The *block instruments*. In some cases there may be one for each line and each direction. In other cases the block indicators for both directions on a pair of lines to and from the same signalbox may be combined in one instrument. Block instruments usually have three indications, known as *positions*: 'Normal' (line blocked), 'Line clear' and 'Train on line'. Block instruments in some parts of the country have reminder equipment attached. There may still be some older types of block instrument in use, dating back to pre-Grouping days, which differ from the above.

2. The *bells*, which convey coded messages from the signalboxes on each side. One bell is provided for each pair of lines to and from one signalbox; therefore at a junction on a four-track section with a two-track branch line there are five bells, each one different in tone.

3. The *tapper keys*, for sending coded messages to, and acknowledging coded messages from, the signalboxes on each side. These keys are sometimes incorporated in the block instrument.

4. The *block switch*, which enables the signalbox to be closed when the line is still open for trains. When the signaller wishes to close the signalbox he sends the appropriate bell signal to the signalbox on each side (7–5–5) and turns the switch. This puts the signalboxes on each side into through communication with each other. He then clears his signals. If the starting signal requires a 'Line clear' release, he sends the bell signal 5–5–7 instead of 7–5–5. The signaller in advance will then move his block indicator to 'Line clear' until he has been informed by one beat on the bell that the signal has been cleared, after which he will restore the block indicator to the 'Normal' position. A signaller may switch out only when there are no trains in the sections concerned and the block indicators are in the 'Normal' (line blocked) position. After the 'Closing' bell signal has been acknowledged, the signallers at each side of the box being switched out must test their indicators and bells. The signaller switching out must be told when all is in order, and he must not leave duty until he has received this information.

5. *Signal-light repeaters*. These instruments are provided for signals out of the signaller's sight, and tell him whether the lights in the signals are *in* (*i.e.* lit) or *out* (not lit for any reason). When a light goes out a buzzer sounds to alert the signaller, who will then take certain precautions regarding the movement of trains and arrange to have the lamps relit. On those signals which are within his sight but have their backs to him, a small aperture, known as a *back light*, is cut in the back of the signal lamp and covered with plain glass so that the signaller can tell whether the lamp is alight or not. He can also tell whether the signal is *on* (*i.e.* at Danger or Caution) or *off* (*i.e.* Clear): when the signal is pulled off, a plate swings over and obscures the back light.

6. *Signal-arm repeaters*. These instruments tell the signaller whether the arms of signals out of his sight are on or off. There is an intermediate position, known as *wrong*, which indicates that the signal may be half-way between on and off, referred to colloquially by railwaymen as 'at half-cock'. The signaller can use the wire-adjuster to tighten or slacken the wire operating the signal and ensure that the signal is properly on or off.

7. *Track-circuit indicators*. If the signalbox does not have an illuminated diagram incorporating the track-circuit indications, separate instruments are provided for each track circuit, which indicate whether the track circuit is occupied or clear. The normal indicator takes the form of a centrally-pivoted black or red rectangle in a white circle. The rectangle is horizontal when the track circuit is occupied, and rotates to 45° when the track circuit is clear.

8. *Sealed releases*. If an item of equipment fails and has the effect of locking points so that they cannot be moved (fail-safe mode) a release is provided in the form of a push-button so that the points can be moved under emergency conditions. The release button is normally covered by paper or glass, so that it cannot be pressed without tearing the paper or breaking the glass, which proves that it has been used. Once broken, the paper seal or glass can only be replaced by a qualified technician. Sealed releases must be used with care by the signaller, as they override the normal built-in safety of the interlocking.

Other equipment in the signalbox is as follows:

1. A large diagram showing the track layout and all the points and signals under the control of the signaller. In some signalboxes, the track-circuit indications are included on the diagram by means of coloured lights, in which case the diagram is referred to as an *illuminated diagram*.

2. A clock, which must be checked and corrected between 09.00 and 10.00 each day. On some lines a time signal is sent at 09.00 from a central point by means of a special code ring on the railway internal telephone circuit.

3. The *Train Register Book*, in which all bell signals sent and received are recorded by time, to the nearest minute, half minutes being rounded up to the next minute. Details must be recorded of any unusual incident, or engineering work. The signaller signs on and off in the Train Register Book beneath the last entry.

4. *Reminder appliances*, which take the form of a metal collar or similar apparatus, to be slipped over a lever handle to remind the signaller not to pull over the lever in certain circumstances (and physically prevent him from doing so), as in the case of failure of equipment, or the presence of an obstruction on the line. Sometimes reminder appliances are provided that are slotted over the block instrument operating handle when a train is detained at the home signal or within the clearing point.

5. Detonators (see Chapter 14). At most signalboxes detonators can be slid onto the rail head from a machine known as a *detonator placer*, which is operated by a lever or handle in the signalbox. These detonator placers can be effective even if the warning of an emergency is received by a signaller when a train is within a few yards of the signalbox. The detonators in the placers are changed on the first Monday of each alternate month.

6. Flags and handlamps, for giving messages and instructions to drivers. There are three types of flag — green, yellow and red — but each lamp is capable of showing all three colours in rotation, together with a fourth, white light.

7. Telephones connected to other signalboxes, offices etc on a railway internal telephone circuit. Signalboxes usually have, additionally, a British Telecom telephone.

Intermediate Block sections

Intermediate Block is an economical means of dividing a block section into two separate sections, thus increasing line capacity. It is also a means of effecting economy by abolishing a signalbox that no longer has any function other than to signal trains straight along the main line. Intermediate block requires a stop signal roughly halfway between two signalboxes, together with an associated distant signal (see diagram below).

Intermediate Block is generally referred to by its initials 'IB'. In the diagram the signaller accepts trains from 'Y' in the normal way and clears his home and starting signals without asking for 'Line clear' from 'B', provided the line is clear to the overlap of the IB home signal. The line is track-circuited throughout from A's starting signal to the end of the safety overlap beyond the IB home signal. When the signaller at 'A' wishes to clear the IB home signal, he offers the train to 'B' in the normal Absolute Block manner.

During fog or falling snow, if both the IB home and distant signals are semaphores, the signaller at 'A' does not clear his starting signal until he has received the 'Train out of section' signal from 'B' for the previous train, and the block indicator is at the normal position. Most IB signals are colour-light signals, however, in which case the above restrictions will not apply.

Automatic sections

Automatic sections are another means of increasing line capacity, or of abolishing

intermediate signalboxes without reducing line capacity. The line between the two signalboxes concerned is track-circuited throughout, and may have one or more intermediate colour-light stop signals, with associated colour-light distant signals (see drawing).

In the diagram the signaller at 'A' accepts trains from 'Y' in the normal way. He clears his starting signal as soon as automatic section No 1 is clear up to and including the overlap of the IB home signal. He does not offer the train to 'B', and the automatic stop signal will clear as soon as automatic section No 2, including overlap, is clear. The signaller does, however, send the normal 'Is line clear?' bell signal, so that the signaller at 'B' knows which class of train is approaching. In such a case, the 'Is line clear?' signal is regarded as a 'Train description' signal. It will be appreciated that Intermediate Block and automatic sections perform similar functions. Automatic sections are rather more expensive, because the line has to be track-circuited throughout.

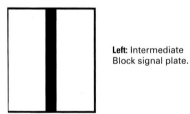

Left: Intermediate Block signal plate.

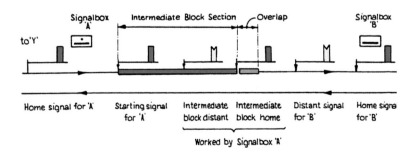

Above: Arrangement of signals and track circuits at an intermediate block section.

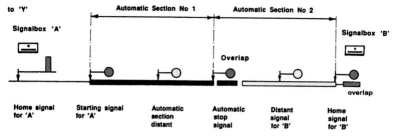

Above: Arrangement of signals and track circuits at an automatic section.

Station working

The Station Working regulations apply within station limits. Station limits apply from the outermost stop signal in the rear to the most advanced stop signal worked from the same signalbox. In effect the signaller is able to make shunting movements, propelling movements and wrong-direction movements without special authority within his 'parish', but requires authority for such movements through or into a block section. Before occupying the overlap with a movement that would come to a stand, however, he must send the 'Blocking back inside home signal' bell signal (2–4) to the signaller in rear, and after the signal has been acknowledged he must move the block indicator to 'Train on line'. If such a movement would occupy the line outside the home signal, that is, in the block section in rear, the bell signal 'Blocking back outside home signal' (3–3) is used instead. Certain conditions must be met before the signaller in rear may give permission for the movement to take place by acknowledging the signal. 'Blocking back' is a safety measure, as it requires the block indicator to be moved to 'Train on line', thus preventing the signaller from accepting another train in a moment of forgetfulness, when his safety overlap is not clear.

Ground frames

A *ground frame* is usually an assembly of levers set in the open on a small wooden platform, with a telephone to the signalbox in rear. The levers are operated by a member of the train crew or a shunter.

Ground frames are provided to operate points in a running line that are too far distant from the signalbox to be worked in the normal way by rodding. The maximum distance for working points by rodding from the signalbox is 350 yards (320m). The points may be trailing ones giving access to a siding, or may form a trailing crossover. It is rare for facing points to be operated from a ground frame, except where provided to facilitate single-line working.

The levers in the ground frame are locked in such a manner that they cannot be used unless certain conditions are fulfilled, and the usual method of operation is as follows (we will call the person operating the points a shunter, for convenience).

When the shunter wishes to operate the ground frame points he telephones the signaller for permission. If the signaller is in a position to give such permission, depending on other train movements, he releases the ground frame by pulling over a lever, which in turn locks his starting signal at Danger. An indicator is provided at the ground frame to show whether it is locked or free; and when it shows 'free' the shunter pulls over a lever, known as a *king lever* because when pulled over it releases the other levers in the ground frame through mechanical interlocking. The shunter is now free to carry out his shunting movements in safety.

When shunting is complete, the shunter restores the points to normal, replaces the king lever and telephones the signaller accordingly.

At some ground frames, the whole train may be set back into the sidings clear of the main line; and in order to ensure safety a track circuit is provided on the main line covering a distance of a maximum train length plus 110 yards (100m) on the approach side of the ground frame points and extending to 220 yarsds (200m) beyond the points. A stop signal may also be provided on the main line, just before the points. It is normally at Clear.

The track-circuit controls the release as follows:

1. For a right-away movement from the siding to the main line, the track circuit must be clear.
2. For a setting-back movement from the main line into the sidings, the track circuit must be occupied for a sufficient time to ensure that the train has come to a stand.

These are the normal arrangements at ground frames, but the arrangements may differ in detail at some individual ground frames, especially where they have been in use for many years.

Above: A ground frame at Fort William, operating points some distance from the signalbox. A release is given by the signaller to enable the points to be operated. *D. C. Hall*

The arrangements for dealing with all types of emergencies and irregularities on Absolute Block lines have been developed and refined over more than a century, usually to incorporate lessons learned from accidents, and they are numerous. This chapter, which is intended as a general guide and summary and is not intended to be comprehensive, deals with the following types of emergency:

● An obstruction on the line
● A train needing to be stopped for examination owing to a defect, etc
● A train taking an unusually long time to pass through a section
● A train passing without a tail lamp
● Protection of the line
● Dealing with a train which has broken down in the section
● Examination of the line
● Failure of the block-signalling equipment

An obstruction on the line

If a signaller becomes aware of an obstruction on the line that might endanger a train, and the obstruction is either in the rear section or in his safety overlap, he must send the 'Obstruction danger' signal (six beats) to the signaller in rear and move his block indicator to 'Train on line' (if it is not already in that position). He must also place or maintain his signals at Danger to protect the obstruction. The 'Obstruction danger' signal must also be sent if it is necessary to prevent the approach of a train from the box in the rear for any other exceptional reason.

The signaller must also send six beats if he sees a train approaching that he has not accepted, or for which he has not received the 'Train entering section' signal; this enables trains to be stopped while the situation is investigated and rectified.

The signaller must then inform the other signaller the reason for sending the signal.

The signaller receiving six beats must immediately take the following action:

1. Put his signals to Danger if they have been cleared.
2. Operate his detonator-placing machine.
3. Acknowledge the six beats.
4. Put three detonators on the obstructed line, 22 yards (20m) apart. (Usually, in

signalboxes that are open continuously, they are hung on a nail near the door for just such an emergency.)
5. Answer the telephone. The other signaller telephones to say why he sent six beats.
6. If he succeeds in stopping a train which is proceeding towards the obstruction he must send the 'Cancelling' signal (3–5). If he is not successful he must at once, without acknowledging the six beats and without sending 'Call attention', send the 'Train running away' signal (4–5–5). The signaller in advance, on receiving the 4–5–5 signal, must do everything he can to stop the approaching train before it hits the obstruction, but there is often little that he can do in the time available.

Animals on the line are not considered to be a sufficient obstruction to justify sending the 'Obstruction danger' signal, but if there are known to be animals on the line, all trains must be stopped so that the drivers can be told about the situation and instructed to proceed cautiously. A train must not enter a tunnel until it has been established that there are no animals in it.

If a driver or guard sees a cow or bull or other large animal within the boundary fence, irrespective of whether trains are immediately in danger, or if either person sees other animals on or near the track and considers that trains may be endangered, he must alert the signaller. The driver must warn the driver of any approaching train by sounding the horn and showing a red light. The driver must also stop his train and place a track-circuit-operating clip and three detonators on the other line at least 1¼ mile (2km) from the animals, except where the signaller has been contacted and has given assurance that it is not necessary.

A train needing to be stopped for examination

A signaller is required to watch each train as it passes, to see whether everything is in order. If anything unusual is seen, such as signals of alarm, goods displaced dangerously or falling off, fire, a hot axlebox, a door open etc he must stop the train if he can, but if not he must send the 'Stop and examine train' signal (seven beats) to the signaller in advance, and telephone him with the reason. This action must also be taken if the signaller becomes aware that the train may have caused damage to the infrastructure. He must also stop trains going the other way unless he is satisfied that there is no need to do so. Automatic means of detecting hot axleboxes are described in Chapter 29.

The signaller receiving seven beats must put all his signals to Danger in both directions, and when the train arrives it must be dealt with as necessary. If nothing can be found, the driver of the next train through the section on any line must be told about it, and instructed to proceed cautiously and report at the next signalbox.

If something is found that cannot be dealt with there and then, the train may be sent forward to a place where it can be dealt with. The train is signalled in the usual way, but after the 'Train entering section' signal has been acknowledged, the 'Stop and examine train' signal must be sent. While being worked forward in this manner, the train must not be passed by another train running on an adjacent line unless it has been established that it can be done safely.

If a signaller sees a door open on a passenger train but there is no report of anyone having fallen from the train, he must tell the signaller in rear, so that the driver of the first train through the section on each line can be sent through at Caution, having been instructed to keep a good lookout. If, however, there is definite information that a passenger *has* fallen from the train, all trains must be detained until the line has been searched.

If the signaller notices or is told that a train is proceeding without showing a headlight, he must arrange for the driver to be made aware. It is better for this to be done at the next signalbox rather than bring the train to a sudden stand.

Train in section for an unusually long time

If a signaller receives the 'Train entering section' signal for a train, and the train then fails to appear at the appropriate time, it is obvious that something is wrong. The train may merely be proceeding more slowly than usual, but on the other hand it may have broken down or, worse still, it may have collided with an obstruction or become derailed. There are many reasons why the train may have stopped, and it is important to find out what has happened. It is also important to stop any other train from proceeding into the section until the driver has been apprised of the situation and instructed to proceed cautiously. During poor visibility, or if there is a tunnel in the section, the line must first be examined (see below) before trains are allowed to run.

The signaller must not accept a train on any line in the same direction until he has told the signaller in rear what has happened. However, if he has already accepted a train but it has not yet entered the section, he must send the 'Train an unusually long time in section' signal (6–2).

Eventually the signaller will discover what has happened, either from a member of the train crew walking to the nearest signalbox or telephoning, or from the driver of the first train passing cautiously through the section. Appropriate action can then be taken.

A train passing without a tail lamp

The signaller must observe the tail-lamp/light before he sends the 'Train out of section' signal. When loose-coupled trains (*i.e.* trains without continuously-coupled power-operated brakes) were common, they not infrequently broke in two, with the rear portion coming to a stand in mid-section and the front portion continuing forward unchecked. It was vital that the signaller became aware of this, through the absence of a tail lamp at the rear of the first portion. If a continuously braked train breaks in two, the parting of the brake pipe normally causes the brakes to be applied automatically, bringing both portions to a stand, possibly in mid-section; but in case the brakes should fail to be applied on the first portion, it is still important for the signaller to look out for the tail lamp.

If a train is seen to pass without a tail lamp, it must be stopped as soon as reasonably practicable. Any train going the other way must also be stopped, and the driver told what has happened and that he must proceed cautiously. The signaller noticing the absence of a tail lamp must send the 'Train passed without tail lamp' signal (nine beats to the signaller in advance, 4–5 to the signaller in rear) and maintain the block indicator at 'Train on line'. During poor visibility, or if there is a tunnel in the section, the line must first be examined (see below) before trains are allowed to run.

If a train passes with its tail lamp in position but unlit when it should be lit, no special action is necessary by the signaller other than to send nine beats to the next signaller and tell him why. The signaller receiving nine beats must stop the train concerned if he can do so without bringing it to a sudden stand, then find out whether it is complete or not and take appropriate action. If stopping the train would entail bringing it to a sudden stand it must be allowed to proceed, and the signaller concerned must pass forward the 'Train passed without tail lamp' signal.

Protection of the line

It is appropriate here to say a few words about the actions of train crews when trains break down or have an accident in mid-section. In theory, the train should be perfectly safe from any risk of another train running into the back of it, because the block signalling system should protect it, but there is always a remote risk that a signaller might make an error and allow another train to enter the section, which would be very dangerous.

An accident may, however, obstruct another line, which will not at that moment be protected by the signalling system, and train crews must take emergency action to secure what is known as *the safety of the line*.

The driver must quickly decide whether any other line is obstructed and use the emergency-call procedure to contact Operations Control by radio. He must also inform the signaller in the quickest way possible, either by radio or from a nearby telephone. If he is unable to contact the signaller direct, he must immediately carry out emergency protection. He must place a track-circuit-operating clip on each line obstructed, then display a red flag or light and place three detonators on the line, 22 yards (20m) apart, 1¼ mile (2km) from the obstruction.

If the driver needs assistance in carrying out emergency protection on other lines he must ask the guard or any other competent person to assist, but if the driver is unable to carry out protection (because he is injured or trapped, for example), the guard must carry out the driver's duties. The guard's first duties, therefore, are to place a track-circuit-operating clip on any obstructed line and then contact the driver. It is desirable for the guard to remain with the train and look after the passengers' welfare if this can be done without delaying protection.

The signaller's role when advised of a train accident is to put his signals to Danger and arrange for a general emergency broadcast to be made by train radio.

This is a very general description of the arrangements for protection of the line, which are set out in great detail in Rule Book Module M1, 'Train stopped by train accident, fire or accidental division'.

A train that has broken down in mid-section

If a train breaks down in mid-section, emergency protection need not be carried out unless the driver is unable to contact the signaller immediately, but some protection is necessary to warn the driver of a locomotive coming to assist that he is getting close to the broken-down train. This is known as *assistance protection*, and involves placing three detonators, 22 yards (20m) apart, 300 yards (274m) from the train in the direction from which help is coming.

The driver must remain at the detonators, ready to conduct the driver of the assisting locomotive to the failed train, and the signaller must not allow the assisting locomotive to enter the section until he knows that the driver of the failed train is in his appointed place or is proceeding to it.

On a number of occasions an assisting locomotive has collided heavily with the failed train, and the instructions are now very precise: 'The driver of the assisting locomotive must proceed very cautiously and look out for the driver of the failed train. The assisting driver must not enter a tunnel unless the failed train driver has been picked up or he is not in the tunnel. The assisting driver must stop on exploding the first detonators (which may be only 300 yards [274m] from the train).'

It will be noted that the guard is not involved in these arrangements; his duty is to remain with the failed train and look after the passengers.

So far as the signaller is concerned, he must tell the assisting driver the exact location of the failed train, how it is protected, and the point from where it will be conducted by the driver of the failed train. The assisting locomotive must not be allowed to enter the section until the signaller has sent the 'Train entering section' signal and it has been acknowledged. After the failed train has been cleared from the section, the next train on that line must also be sent through cautiously.

If the failed train is cleared from the section either by being drawn back to the signalbox in rear, or by being hauled to the signalbox in advance, there is a danger that part of it may accidentally have been left behind. To deal with that situation the block indicator must be maintained at 'Train on line', and the driver of the next train that is to pass through the section on that line must be cautioned and told to pass the section signal at Danger.

The term 'assisting locomotive' has been used for simplicity, but any type of train that is suitable may be used to clear a failed train from a section. If there is no siding accommodation at the signalbox in advance, the two trains may continue forward together as far as is necessary.

Examination of the line

The phrase 'examination of the line' must be interpreted in its widest sense of looking to see whether everything is safe for trains to proceed normally. The arrangements are very similar to those set out in Chapter 10 for track-circuit block, but the signalling of the train is somewhat different. The signallers concerned must be able to speak to each other, and the 'Train out of section' signal must have been received for the previous train. The signaller in rear does not send the 'Is line clear' signal for the examining train, but tells his colleague at the next signalbox what class of train it is, and sends only the 'Train entering section' signal. The driver of the examining train must be told by the signaller to pass the section signal at danger and proceed at caution.

Any class of train, including a passenger train, may be used to examine the line, and it is not necessary for the driver to be accompanied during darkness, fog or falling snow, nor if the affected portion of line is within a tunnel, unless the guard or other competent person is immediately available. However, the driver must not proceed through the tunnel at more than 10mph. If definite information has been received that someone has fallen from a train, the driver must be accompanied during darkness, fog or falling snow, or within a tunnel.

The arrangements for dealing with track circuit failures and suspected track defects are also very similar to those set out in Chapter 10 and need not be repeated here.

Failure of the block signalling equipment

Occasionally the block signalling equipment does not work correctly, often owing to an interruption in the telegraph wire or cable between two signalboxes. When this happens, the failure may affect the bells or the block instruments or both. If a telephone is available, it may be used to pass signalling messages, but if a telephone is not available, steps must be taken to obtain a replacement form of communication, such as radio. If the signaller can see that the section is clear, however, trains may be allowed to pass through. The 'time interval' method of working, which was in operation for many years, is no longer used.

If only the bells have failed, but the block indicators are being worked in conjunction with telephone messages, the driver of the first train to pass through the affected section must be advised of the circumstances and instructed to proceed cautiously. In all other cases, the signaller must explain the circumstances to the driver intending to proceed into the section where the failure exists, and instruct him to pass the section signal at Danger and proceed cautiously. The driver of the first train travelling on each adjacent line must be advised of the circumstances and told to proceed cautiously through the section.

PART 4

Signals are the means by which the driver receives his instructions from the signaller. In addition to Stop, Caution and Clear, however, there are other factors to be considered if safety is to be achieved.

The term 'guard' is synonymous with 'conductor' etc.

Observance of signals

When a train stops on the approach to a signal showing a Proceed aspect (at a station platform, for example) the driver must look at the signal again before restarting, in case the signaller has replaced it to Danger in the meantime either in an emergency or to give priority to another train. In the latter case the signaller must not clear his signals for a conflicting movement until he is sure that the driver of the first train has noticed that the signal has been replaced.

If a driver finds that a junction signal is cleared for the wrong route he must stop at the signal if it is safe and practicable to do so, and speak to the signaller.

If a train is stopped, or nearly stopped, before the clearance of a stop signal (other than a multiple-aspect colour-light), this may be a warning to the driver that the next signal is also at Danger. The signals are worked in this way in order to avoid any risk of the driver's failing to observe the next signal, should it be at Danger. When a train is stopped or nearly stopped in this manner, the driver must also look to see whether the signaller requires him to stop at the signalbox.

Doubt as to signal aspect

In the following circumstances a driver must treat a stop signal as being at Danger (or a distant signal at Caution):

- No signal, where there should be one
- No light in a signal
- A colour-light signal, if there is doubt as to which aspect applies
- A semaphore signal at 'half-cock' (neither on nor off). (After dark this may cause a part green/part red light to be displayed.)

- A white light where there should be a coloured light.

The driver must immediately inform the signaller, stopping specially to do so, if necessary. He must also do so if he sees any irregularity in the working of signals, or an irregular aspect sequence, and complete the appropriate report form.

Being authorised to pass a signal at Danger

There are several circumstances in which this may occur, the authority being given personally to the driver by the signaller or other nominated person. Before starting the driver must reset the Driver's Reminder Appliance (Chapter 24), press the TPWS override button (if the signal is fitted with TPWS), give one long blast on the horn, then proceed cautiously at such reduced speed as will enable him to stop the train clear of any obstruction. The driver must always be able to stop within the distance he can see the line to be clear; it is better to incur delay than risk a collision.

The driver must observe any facing points to see that they are in the correct position, and pass through them at not more than 15mph (24km/h).

If the driver sees the next stop signal ahead showing a Proceed aspect, he must not assume that it is meant for him. It may be for a train in front.

Train detained at a signal at Danger

A train standing at a signal could be in danger if its presence is forgotten by the signaller, unless a track circuit is provided. As a safeguard, therefore, if a track circuit is not provided, the driver must go to the signalbox to remind the signaller that the train is there. In colour-light areas, although track circuits or axle counters are provided it is still necessary for the driver to speak to the signaller in case the latter wishes to give him a message. The detailed requirements are as follows.

1.   Where there is a telephone at the signal (indicated by a black and white diagonal striped sign) the driver must speak to the

signaller immediately where indicated at the signal, or otherwise within 2 minutes, and then at intervals of 5 minutes if he is still detained. He must use the telephone to do this unless GSM-R radio or cab secure radio is available (see Chapter 32), in which case these methods should be used instead. At some signals the driver is allowed to wait more than 2 minutes before he makes his initial call, in which case the number of minutes is given on the black and white sign.

2. Where there is a yellow diamond sign with the letter 'T' at the signal, the driver need not speak to the signaller unless an associated white flashing light is displayed. This means in effect that the signaller has a message for the driver.

3. Where there is a yellow or white diamond sign with the letter 'X' at the signal, or where there is a sign on the telephone cabinet showing a black cross on a white background with a yellow roundel superimposed on it, the driver must not leave his cab to use the telephone except in emergency; he must use his radio or mobile telephone to contact the signaller, but if neither is available, he must stay in his cab until the signal clears or until someone tells him that the next line has been blocked by the signaller and it is safe for him to leave his cab to use the telephone. This procedure is in force at places where there are several running lines close together and the driver would be in danger if he left his cab to use the telephone.

4.(a) If there is no telephone at the signal, the driver must sound the horn as soon as he comes to a stand. If there is a white diamond sign at the signal, the presence of the train is detected by a track circuit. The driver should contact the signaller using the GSM-R radio system, cab secure radio system or, if these are not available, the National Radio Network radio or driver's mobile telephone. If the driver still cannot contact the signaller, he should either find a signal or lineside telephone or go to the signalbox if the train is detained for an unusually long time (after not more than 10 minutes in all cases). In some cases the telephone number of the signalbox is displayed on a plate on the signal post.

4.(b) If there is no white diamond sign at the signal, the driver must attempt to contact the signaller using the appropriate means, failing which he must go to the signalbox within 2 minutes in clear weather, or immediately in fog or falling snow. When a section signal without a white diamond sign is at Danger, the driver must not draw forward to stand at it, as he would then have to walk back to the signalbox to remind the signaller about the standing train, but must stop his train as close as possible to the signalbox (well clear of any junction) so that the train is within the signaller's sight and the driver can reach the signalbox quickly and easily.

Actions of the signaller and driver

When a driver enters a signalbox to remind the signaller about his train standing on the main line, he must write in the Train Register Book 'Train No … detained on … line at … signal', together with the time. Both persons must sign the entry, and the driver must remain in the signalbox to act as a reminder to the signaller, unless the signaller assures him that he has used the reminder appliances (*e.g.* by putting a lever collar on the signal in rear of the standing train).

Failure of telephone at a signal

If a train is detained at an automatic signal, a semi-automatic signal or an Intermediate Block home signal, and the driver finds that the telephone has failed and he cannot make contact by the train's radio or mobile telephone, he must take his train past the signal at Danger and proceed very cautiously to the next stop signal, taking special care at any points. He must then stop at the next signal, whether it is showing a Proceed aspect or not, and try again to speak to the signaller. If unsuccessful he must repeat the above procedure at the types of signals mentioned, as many times as necessary.

At any other type of signal the driver must speak to the signaller the best way he can, but if it is not practicable for him to do so he must go to the signalbox.

If the train is detained at a controlled signal, the driver must contact the signaller by radio, or by using the telephone at another signal, or using a lineside telephone or his mobile telephone. If none of these is available the driver must go to the signalbox.

Driver's reminder appliance

Drivers have long been aware of the possibility of inadvertently starting away against platform starting signals at Danger, caused in part by the incorrect receipt of the 'Ready to start' bell signal from the guard, and some drivers had their own method of reminding themselves that the platform starting signal was at Danger. This has now been regularised by the provision of a reminder appliance in the form of a large button. When depressed, the button illuminates red and prevents traction power from being applied until the button is pulled out. In this form the device is known as the *Driver's Reminder Appliance* (DRA), and is fitted to the drivers' cabs of all passenger trains.

The DRA must be set whenever a train stops at a signal at Danger, and reset when the signal clears. It must also be set when the train stops at a station where no signal is provided, after the train has passed the previous signal when at Caution. This is to remind the driver that the signal ahead (which may be out of sight) may still be at Danger. In a few trains, the DRA sets automatically. DRA is described further in Chapter 24.

The standard Automatic Warning System was approved for use on British Railways in 1956, since when it has been installed on almost all Britain's total route mileage of approximately 10,000 miles. Its simple purpose is to remind a driver that he needs to slow down or stop. If he fails to acknowledge such a reminder, the brakes will be applied automatically within two or three seconds.

Track equipment
A permanent magnet and an electromagnet are installed between the rails — the position known as the *four-foot*, historically the *four-foot way*), normally about 200 yards (180m) on the approach side of signals that can display a Caution or Preliminary Caution aspect. The distance is increased to 260 yards (230m) where permissible speeds are greater than 100mph (160km/h). At certain locations a suppressible magnet may be provided beyond the signal.

A permanent magnet only is provided on the approach to permanent speed restriction warning boards (sometimes known as *Morpeth* boards, following a serious accident there in 1969) where the approach speed is greater than 60mph (96km/h) and the reduction in speed required is a third or more. Portable permanent magnets are also installed on the approach to temporary speed restrictions and emergency speed restrictions.

Locomotive or multiple-unit equipment
A receiver is fixed underneath each end of a locomotive or multiple-unit, and it reacts to the magnets fixed in the track. A bell and a horn (or an electronic representation) are provided in the cab, together with an acknowledgement button and a visual indicator.

Method of operation
When a signal displays a Clear aspect, the electromagnet is energised. This causes the bell in the driving cab to give a short ring, and the visual indicator to show all-black. No action is required of the driver.

In all other cases the electromagnet is inoperative. When a train passes over the permanent magnet the horn sounds a warning, and unless the driver presses the acknowledgement button within 2-3 seconds (which silences the horn) an emergency application of the brake will be made. The visual indicator shows all-black until the acknowledgement button is pressed, after which it

will display a segmented disc, coloured alternately black and yellow, as a reminder to the driver that he has acknowledged a warning and has overridden the automatic brake application. The responsibility for applying the brake is now the driver's.

Summary of warnings
Where AWS equipment is provided, the warning horn sounds when the train is approaching the following:

1. A colour-light signal displaying any of these aspects: red, single yellow, double yellow, flashing single yellow and flashing double yellow
2. A semaphore signal at Caution
3. A warning sign of a permanent speed restriction
4. A warning sign of a temporary speed restriction
5. A warning sign of a speed restriction imposed without notice in an emergency
6. A cancelling indicator on a single line for trains moving in the opposite direction to which the signal applies
7. A warning board in connection with two types of automatic level crossing, ABCL (see Chapter 27) and AOCL (Chapter 28), where the train driver has to check that the flashing red road traffic signals are working properly before he takes his train over the crossing
8. A signal displaying a Clear aspect, alongside which has been placed a warning sign or indicator referring to a temporary or emergency speed restriction
9. A splitting distant signal that is at Clear for the diverging route.

AWS gaps
At many large stations where speeds are low, AWS equipment is not provided, even though the approach lines are equipped. The start of the AWS gap is indicated by a circular white sign showing 'AWS' with a red cross. The end is indicated by a square white sign showing 'AWS'.

In some places, AWS equipment is not provided for trains travelling in the wrong direction on a bidirectional line. The start of the AWS gap is indicated by a diamond-shaped white sign showing 'AWS' with a red cross. The end is indicated by the same sign without the red cross.

Above: An archive photograph illustrating trials of the BR Automatic Warning System in the 1950s, showing the magnets between the two rails, and the receiver underneath the locomotive directly above the magnets. The locomotive is LNER Class A4 Pacific No 60007 *Sir Nigel Gresley*.
Ian Allan Library

Failures and irregularities

If the bell sounds in circumstances in which the horn should sound (or if there is no sound), there is a misleading failure, known as a *wrong-side failure*, and the driver must tell the signaller at once, stopping specially if necessary, so that other drivers can be warned.

If there is a right-side failure (a horn, or no indication, when there should have been a bell) the driver must tell the signaller at the first convenient opportunity, so that the defect can be repaired.

AWS isolation

A locomotive or unit must not enter service if the AWS is isolated (*i.e.* out of use) in any driving cab that is required to be used, or if the seal is broken on an AWS isolating handle. Here the meaning of the term 'in service' has been modified to denote a train that is ready to start a journey; it no longer means entering service from a depot. A train is out of service at the end of a journey or reversing point. The term 'journey' means a journey between a station, depot or siding and another station, depot or siding. A journey finishes where a train has to reverse or is to have vehicles attached or detached.

Above: Sign denoting that AWS does not apply to trains travelling in that direction on a single line.

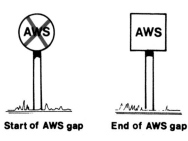

Start of AWS gap   **End of AWS gap**

Above: Signs showing the start and finish of AWS gaps, usually at a low-speed station.

Below: Signs showing the start and finish of AWS gaps for trains travelling in the wrong direction on a bi-directional line.

   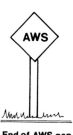

Start of AWS gap   **End of AWS gap**

If, while in service, the pressing of the acknowledgement button does not stop the sounding of the horn, or does not prevent the brakes from being applied, the driver must isolate the AWS. He must then tell the signaller and not move the train until instructed to do so. The signaller must tell Operations Control at once.

The driver will be told of the arrangements that are being made. If a competent person is available to accompany the driver and stop the train in an emergency, the train may proceed normally to a nominated point. If no such person is available, the train may proceed to a nominated point at a maximum speed of 40mph (64km/h).

Very detailed and comprehensive instructions for dealing with AWS failures arose following the serious accident at Southall on 19 September 1997 in which the AWS was isolated in the leading cab and in which six people were killed. The instructions are contained in Rule Book Module TW5, 'Preparation and movement of trains. Defective or isolated vehicles and on-train equipment'.

The Train Protection & Warning System (TPWS) was developed as an enhancement of AWS when it was decided not to proceed with Automatic Train Protection (see Chapter 21). TPWS does not prevent signals from being passed at Danger, but is designed to reduce the possible consequences if such an event occurs. It is designed to cover the eventuality of a driver's acknowledging the AWS warning at a Caution signal and then failing to apply the brake. It also incorporates a train stop that applies the brake immediately if a driver passes a signal at Danger, which is a very valuable safeguard in the case of platform starting signals. TPWS is also provided on the approach to buffer stops at passenger platforms, and on the approach to permanent speed restrictions where the approach speed is 60mph (96km/h) or more and the reduction in speed is at least one third (*i.e.* those that are provided with permanent AWS magnets).

TPWS does not provide the same degree of protection as ATP, but it had the great benefit of being able to be installed within a much shorter timescale and at a much lower cost. It is a legal requirement that TPWS be provided at all high-risk signals, *i.e.* those protecting crossovers and areas of conflicting movement, which covers about 40% of the total number of signals. Experience has shown that these are the signals most likely to result in accidents. Following the very serious collision at Ladbroke Grove on 5 October 1999, which was caused by a SPAD (signal passed at Danger without authority), there was an urgency to have TPWS installed as soon as possible, and Railtrack achieved this by the end of 2002, a year before the Regulations required it. Where TPWS is installed the existing AWS continues to operate normally.

Track equipment

The track equipment consists of an overspeed sensor (known as a *speed trap*) on the approach to a signal, and a *train-stop sensor* at a signal.

The overspeed sensor

The overspeed sensor initiates an emergency brake application if a train approaches a TPWS-

Right: TPWS grids next to AWS magnets.
Author

fitted signal at Danger at such a speed that the signal is likely to be passed. The precise location of the overspeed sensor and its speed setting depends on the gradient and certain features regarding the track and signalling layout ahead, but is likely to be within the range 100-500 yards (90-450m) before the signal. It will be remembered that there is normally at least a 200 yards (180m) overlap beyond multiple-aspect colour-light signals, and TPWS should ensure that a train with good braking characteristics (at least 12% g) that is travelling at up to 75mph (120km/h) and has triggered the overspeed sensor will be stopped within the overlap.

In many cases protection will be effective for approach speeds greater than 75mph (120km/h) and braking worse than 12% g because the junction ahead where conflicting movements can occur is further from the signal than the overlap distance. This distance is called the *safe overrun distance*.

The sensor consists of an *arming loop* and a *trigger loop*. The arming loop causes a timer to be started in the TPWS equipment on the train, and if the trigger loop is reached before the timer has expired, an emergency brake application will result. Different timer settings are used on freight locomotives to enhance the effectiveness of TPWS, since their braking capabilities are poorer than those of passenger trains.

The train-stop sensor

The train-stop sensor initiates an emergency brake application if the train passes a TPWS-equipped signal at Danger. An override device is provided to inhibit the operation of the brake if the driver is authorised to pass the signal at Danger.

Train-borne equipment

The train-borne equipment consists of an aerial located underneath the traction unit, together with a TPWS electronics unit incorporating the AWS equipment.

Operation of TPWS

TPWS may operate on the approach to a signal at Danger while the driver is already braking, in which case it is known as an *activation*. Where a driver is not already braking, the operation of TPWS is known as an *intervention*. In addition to

the immediate emergency brake application, the operation of TPWS causes an AWS warning to occur and a red indicator light known as a *brake-demand light* to flash on the TPWS panel in the driver's cab.

One weakness of TPWS is that, once having come to a stand, the driver can reset the system and carry on. He may do this if he does not realise that a TPWS operation has occurred, or if he mistakenly believes that he needs to clear a junction that he may have stopped foul of. To counter this, the instructions are very clear that a driver must always consider that an emergency brake application could be caused by operation of the TPWS and that he should not move the train afterwards without the permission of the signaller.

Increasing the level of protection given by TPWS

TPWS has also been fitted to a few plain-line signals that do not protect junctions that have been specifically identified as being higher risk. They may include signals that protect level crossings where there is sufficient overrun distance to provide protection.

Protection for train speeds in excess of 75mph (120km/h) can be obtained by providing an additional overspeed sensor further back from the signal. This is known as TPWS+.

If TPWS+ is insufficient to stop a train in the safe overrun distance, the level of protection can be increased further by fitting additional TPWS to the signal in rear of the one that protects the junction (the junction-protecting signal). This (outer) signal is then controlled so that it will show an unrestricted Proceed aspect only if the route is set forward from the junction protecting signal, or if the train has slowed down sufficiently on the approach to the outer signal to be considered to be under control, in which case the outer signal will clear to allow the train to move up to the junction-protecting signal.

Where there are facing points beyond the junction protecting signal, the safe overrun distance can be increased by altering the signalling controls so that any train overrunning the signal is diverted along a route where the consequences are likely to be least severe; this is known as *flank protection*.

Automatic Train Protection, known as ATP, is a more sophisticated system than the Automatic Warning System (AWS) and the Train Protection & Warning System (TPWS) described in Chapters 19 and 20. AWS warns the driver when he needs to reduce speed or stop, either for a speed restriction or a signal at Danger. Furthermore, it checks that the driver has actually received the warning, because unless he acknowledges the warning by pressing a button, the brakes are applied automatically. TPWS is fitted to those signals that have been identified as highest risk, but the degree of protection given depends on the distance to the point where conflicting movements can occur, as well as the approach speed and a train's braking capability. There is also nothing to stop a driver continuing once he has been stopped after the operation of TPWS.

AWS has been invaluable in raising safety standards on Britain's railways, but it is not designed to check that the driver is actually responding to the warning he has acknowledged and that he is applying the brakes appropriately. It might be thought that such provision would be unnecessary, on the grounds that if a driver is sufficiently alert to acknowledge receiving the warning by the physical act of pressing a button, he is sufficiently alert to apply the brakes. However, there is now a substantial body of experience to show that this is not always the case, and several serious accidents have occurred in which drivers have pressed the acknowledgement button but have then failed to brake correctly, or even at all.

Since TPWS was installed, the level of protection against SPADs has been raised substantially and it is almost certainly the case that a number of collisions have been avoided because a signal that was passed at Danger was fitted with TPWS. The weaknesses of TPWS have been mentioned earlier.

ATP does not have the weaknesses of AWS and TPWS. Two pilot ATP schemes were introduced in 1991, from different manufacturers, one on the Great Western main line between Paddington and Bristol, and a second on the Chiltern line from Marylebone to Aynho Junction. The trials were more technically demanding, costly and prolonged than had been expected, and eventually it was decided in 1995 by the then Secretary of State for Transport that ATP should not be extended to other routes, on the grounds that the expenditure was not justified — that is, that it would not be cost-effective. The system ought properly to be described as the BR-

ATP system, as it differs in some respects from the subsequently developed European Train Control System (see Chapter 22). Attention was then concentrated on developing TPWS instead.

Initially, BR-ATP works in a similar way to AWS and TPWS. The train picks up messages from the track electronically, which tell the driver that he needs to slow down or stop. But the ATP system then goes on to check that the driver is actually reducing speed to the extent required. If it finds that he is failing to do so, it reminds the driver by giving a short visual and audible warning, and if this warning goes unheeded by the driver ATP will apply the brakes.

This back-check is performed by an on-board computer which, on receipt of the warning, calculates the rate of deceleration (known as the *braking curve*) that would be necessary to bring the train safely to a stand at a signal at Danger (or to reduce the speed to the level required by a speed restriction). The computer continuously checks the actual speed of the train against the braking curve that it has calculated, and gives a warning if it finds that the actual speed is higher than that demanded by the braking curve, followed if necessary by an application of the brake. A distance-measuring tachometer enables the computer to calculate the location of the train relative to the approaching signal.

ATP also safeguards the maximum permitted train speed throughout the journey by monitoring the actual train speed and checking it against the permitted speed. If the permitted speed is exceeded, ATP intervenes to cause speed to be reduced.

Track equipment

At each signal, or at braking distance from a speed restriction, transmitters called *beacons* or *loops* (*balises*) are laid in the track, and transmit the following information to the train via a receiver antenna fixed underneath the locomotive or multiple-unit:

● The distance to the next signal at Danger, or to a speed restriction
● The current maximum permitted speed at the beacon
● The value and length of the next speed restriction, if there is one
● The gradient

Above: ATP speedometer in the cab of an HST. Despite the capability of the instrument, a sign above it reads 'Max. speed 125mph'. *Author*

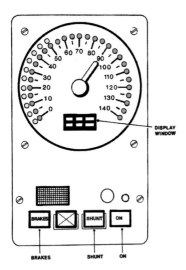

Above: ATP speedometer showing green LEDs and yellow LEDs around the periphery.

Setting the on-board computer

Certain information on board trains that does not alter their performance may be permanently programmed, such as the length and maximum permitted speed of a multiple-unit. In other cases, before starting the journey, the driver inputs the maximum permitted speed of the train, its type, length and braking capability. This information, together with the information received from beacons, enables the on-board computer to calculate the appropriate braking curve.

Cab display

The main item of cab display is the ATP speedometer. Around the periphery of the dial are green light-emitting diodes (LEDs) at 5mph (8km/h) intervals, any one of which may be illuminated to show the maximum permitted speed, or flash to show a target speed ahead. Alongside these, from 0mph to 50mph (80km/h), are yellow LEDs, which have a 'release speed' function. A display window in the speedometer gives the driver a form of 'countdown' to the signal at Danger. See the photograph alongside.

Method of operation

When the train is approaching a double-yellow signal, the green LED display, showing the maximum permitted speed, will change to a single flashing green LED at 0mph, and a short 'blip' tone will sound. The display window will show '0', meaning 'Stop at the next signal but two'. When the train passes the double yellow signal the display window will change to '00', meaning 'Stop at the next signal but one'. When the train passes the single yellow signal, the display window will change to '000', meaning 'Stop at the next signal'.

Throughout this process the train's actual speed is compared with the braking curve calculated by the computer. If the driver fails to brake sufficiently, a warble tone will sound, the indicator in the display window will flash, and the green LED will go out. If the driver allows the ATP system to interpose and apply the brakes he will be unable release them until speed has been reduced to 40mph (64km/h).

As far as speed restrictions are concerned, the procedure is somewhat similar. Approaching a speed restriction, say 40mph (64km/h), the steady green LED showing the maximum permitted speed will be replaced by a flashing green 40mph (64km/h) LED display, and a short 'blip' tone will sound. If the driver brakes correctly, the flashing LED will change to a steady 40mph

(64km/h) display at the start of the speed restriction, and this indication will be maintained until the rear of the train has cleared the end of the speed restriction (hence the need for the driver to input the length of the train).

In order to carry out its functions without constantly interfering with the driver's handling of the train, the on-board ATP computer calculates three curves — the braking curve, the *warning curve* and the *intervention curve*. The warning curve, which gives a visual and audible warning to the driver when its speed is exceeded, has a tolerance of 3mph above the braking curve. Similarly, the intervention curve has a 3mph tolerance above the warning curve, and will apply the brakes if this is exceeded. The curves are calculated to achieve the required speed at the beginning of a speed restriction, or to bring the train safely to a stand in the case of a signal being at Danger.

Track equipment — placed intermittently or laid continuously

The main advantage of continuously-laid track equipment is that it updates the signal information the instant an aspect changes. This means that the driver can start to accelerate as soon as a signal ahead changes to a less restrictive aspect, even though he may not be able to see it. It also provides an added safeguard if a signal out of sight changes to a more restrictive aspect in an emergency; it gives the driver more time to stop. The main disadvantage of continuously-laid track equipment is its cost.

Intermittent track equipment is cheaper, but if it is provided only at signals and speed restrictions, the computer is not updated until the next beacon, and the signal ahead may be in the driver's view for a considerable distance. If the driver has just passed a single yellow signal when the signal ahead changes from red to a Proceed aspect, the driver cannot accelerate but must continue to brake as though the signal were still at red, because that is what the on-board computer still believes. Such slow running may

not be acceptable in heavily worked areas, especially at junctions.

These delays can be reduced in two ways:

1. By providing additional 'fill-in' beacons between signals at critical locations, so that the computer can be updated sooner
2. By allowing the driver to override the computer when he sees the signal ahead change from red, and speed has been reduced to a sufficiently low level, known as the *release speed*. This may appear to be less than entirely satisfactory from a safety point of view, but the release speed chosen for Britain's railways is sufficiently low that a train can be stopped safely within the overlap of the signal at red, should the driver attempt to go past it in error. If the train were to pass a red signal, an immediate brake application would result. The release speed is indicated on the speedometer by the illumination of a yellow LED.

If a driver is required to pass a red signal in an emergency, or because the signal has failed, he can override the ATP system by pressing a special button, but this action will be effective only if the train is stationary at the signal when the button is pressed. When a driver proceeds past a red signal in such a manner the train's speed will be held at 20mph (32km/h) for 3 minutes, unless he passes over another beacon within that time.

Since the accident at Southall in 1997 (when the ATP system fitted to a train which passed a signal at Danger had been switched off), the BR-ATP system has been made a permanent installation on the Great Western and Chiltern lines pending its replacement by the European Train Control System (see Chapter 22). It has also been installed on the Heathrow Express route and trains. It is not intended to install the BR-ATP system elsewhere.

The European Rail Traffic Management System (ERTMS) and the European Train Control System (ETCS) resulted from European Commission Council Directive 96/48/EC of 23 July 1996, concerning the interoperability of the trans-European high-speed rail network. It was designed to provide a single standard train control system on that network to simplify through working from one country to another, and through a country, and to avoid all the complications that have arisen from the many different systems of signalling and train control in use at present in the countries of the European Union.

The term 'train control' is a rather comprehensive phrase dating back at least a century to the Great Western Railway's Automatic Train Control, so called because it could cause the brakes to be applied without any action on the part of the driver. The designers of BR-AWS deliberately avoided using the term 'control', in case it should be interpreted as controlling the speed of the train, both upwards and downwards; it only initiated the braking action. The ATP element of ETCS also initiates the brake action, but train control includes the manner in which instructions are given to the driver, whether by lineside signals or by cab signals or in any other manner. Train control, so far as ETCS is concerned, does not control the driving of the train; that remains with the driver. ETCS intervenes only if the speed is too high in any given circumstance.

The term 'high-speed line' denotes lines with speeds of 125mph (200km/h) and above, and in Britain includes the West Coast and East Coast main lines, the Great Western main line and the Channel Tunnel Rail Link, now known as High Speed 1. As a second stage it is likely that 100mph (160km/h) lines and above will fall within the ETCS requirements. Ultimately, ETCS will enable a train passing through many national administration areas to be equipped with ETCS only. As an example of the present situation, Eurostar trains have to carry five sets of train-control equipment.

A second advantage of a common ETCS system is that it will enable the European train control manufacturing industry to adopt a common specification, which should lead to a cheaper and more reliable product from the various competing train control equipment manufacturers.

ETCS has been fitted to several routes in continental Europe, notably in Switzerland, where there is a plan to equip the entire network.

ETCS variants

These are known as *Levels 1, 2 and 3*, Level 1 being the simplest and Level 3 the most advanced. Levels 2 and 3 use radio instead of cable as a means of communication. A radio project was started some years ago, known as the *European Integrated Railways Radio Enhanced Network* (EIRENE), to develop a radio system capable of carrying data for train control. This work resulted in the development of the Global System for Mobile Communications — Railways (GSM-R) and work is ongoing to fit the British railway network with this system. The aims of the European Union and the European railways are to deliver a high-speed European-wide railway network equipped with ERTMS/ETCS and GSM-R. So far as Britain is concerned, the main benefit is likely to arise from speedier transits of freight across Europe to and from Britain, improving Britain's rail freight companies' competitive position with respect to road transport.

ETCS Level 1

ETCS Level 1 is designed to be applied to a conventional line having lineside signals. Data is stored in balises (lineside transponders) linked to the signalling system. The control centre transmits movement authorities to the on-board computer via the balises, and this enables the computer to calculate speed and braking curves for train protection purposes. The system provides continuous speed supervision and SPAD protection. Additional balises can be installed on the approach to signals to provide updated information.

ETCS Level 1 is the cheapest option, and provides Automatic Train Protection only. Lineside signals and conventional train detection systems (track circuits and axle counters) continue to be used. In practice, Level 1 is the ETCS version of BR-ATP, but there are technical differences.

ETCS Level 2

With ETCS Level 2 lineside signals are not necessary, as all the information that the driver needs is relayed to him by a secure radio system, GSM-R, and displayed on the driving cab console. Conventional train detection systems continue to be used. Lineside signals may, however, be retained in certain circumstances — to allow trains not equipped with ETCS to use the line concerned, and to provide a fallback safeguard in case of failure of the radio control system. Level 2 remains a fixed-block system and includes ATP.

At the time of writing, the Level 2 variant of ETCS was being installed on the Cambrian lines between Shrewsbury, Aberystwyth and Pwllheli as a prototype for more widespread application on the British network.

ETCS Level 3

In ETCS Level 3 lineside signals and conventional train detection systems are not used. The train's position is continuously calculated on board and transmitted to the control centre by secure radio links. Level 3 provides the option of 'moving block' in which trains can follow each other at braking distance apart, but this refinement is not likely to be available for some years, since no work on the development of Level 3 is being carried out at present.

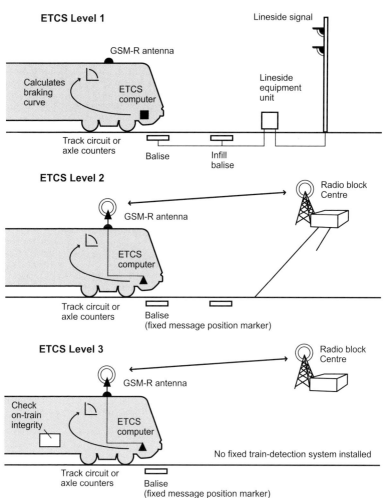

On the West Coast main line tilting trains (Class 390 'Pendolinos' and Class 221 'Super Voyagers') have been authorised to run at speeds above the normal maximum permissible speeds allowed for non-tilting trains, except at large stations and on the slow lines. These speeds are referred to as *enhanced permissible speeds* (EPS) and are designated by special lineside signs.

Trains must not be allowed to tilt in areas where clearances are tight, or to be driven so fast as to create the risk of derailment or overturning. A new protection system was therefore devised and supplied by Alstom, known as the *tilt-authorisation and speed-supervision system*

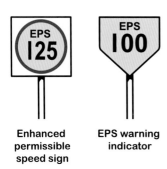

Enhanced permissible speed sign   **EPS warning indicator**

(TASS). Such a system is not required elsewhere in Europe where tilting trains run, because of the more generous loading-gauge in those countries.

TASS is based on a simplified version of the European Train Control System (ETCS), and the equipment on the trains (a vital computer operating on a two-out-of-three majority voting system) is installed in the space provided for the ETCS equipment.

The TASS trackside equipment consists of free-standing *Eurobalises*, needing no power supply, located in the four-foot about every 3 miles (5km). They are programmed with information about the speed profile of the route ahead and whether or not the train is authorised to tilt. A tilting train picks up this information as it passes over a balise, and the information is continually updated as the train passes over successive balises.

TASS should be invisible to the driver in normal circumstances and will intervene to apply the brakes and reduce the speed of the train only if the driver exceeds the enhanced permissible speed.

In the 1970s signalling for BR's Advanced Passenger Train (APT) required that the entire length of the West Coast main line be fitted with balises, which transmitted permissible-speed information to the APT driver.

During the 1990s there was growing concern about the number of instances of signals being passed at Danger. This was given emphasis by the collisions at Southall in 1997 and at Ladbroke Grove in 1999, and by the increase, albeit slight, in the number of SPADs in 1998/9. Several initiatives were therefore taken to improve the position, and since then the number of SPADs has reduced very considerably.

The most significant initiative was the fitment of TPWS to the signals at highest risk, as described in Chapter 20. Other initiatives included improved techniques in sighting signals and in the training of drivers. Train-operating companies introduced 'defensive driving' policies requiring, for example, that drivers positively brake at the first cautionary signal aspect, reduce speed to 20mph (32km/h) by the time they reach the AWS magnets and stop 22 yards (20m) before a signal at Danger. These measures are now deemed to be an inherent part of professional driving. There have also been major improvements to the way that drivers acquire route knowledge, including those features along the route that a driver must particularly note, such as a signal with a poor SPAD record.

A number of steps were also taken to warn drivers that they were approaching a signal of which they did not have a good view on approach and which they may come upon quite suddenly. In a number of cases, banner repeating signals, signs warning of a signal ahead and countdown markers of the type used on the approach to motorway exits have been provided.

Signal sighting

Signal sighting (the driver's approach view of signals) is a very important factor when determining the precise location of new signals, and for investigating the reasons why a signal has been passed at Danger, possibly repeatedly. It is equally important when changes in the surroundings of signals may impede the driver's view of signals. Such changes may result from, for example, building work, the growth of lineside vegetation and the installation of overhead electrification.

Signal siting is the expression used to denote where the signals are located.

When approaching a signal a driver has to interpret the aspects displayed in order to control the train accordingly. Complex signal arrangements such as gantries take longer to assess, leading to the concept of *reading time*. The current standard is for signals to have a minimum reading time, which for a simple lineside signal is generally 8 seconds (less in certain circumstances) when approaching at line speed. This means that the driver must be able to see the signal at least 8 seconds before passing it. The more complicated the signalling arrangement, the greater is the minimum reading time that must be provided. Part of the process of signal sighting is to determine the minimum reading time and assess how it should be provided in practice. Where it is reasonable to do so, the minimum reading time should be increased further if this can be achieved easily, for example by the removal of lineside vegetation.

Signal sighting is carried out by committees set up for the purpose. They must determine exactly where new signals should be sited, and whether any changes should be made to existing signals whose sighting is in question for any reason. A committee consists of a chairman and a number of people who are competent in engineering and train driver requirements, including a competent representative of a train operating company operating over the route.

Sighting considerations are paramount, and the following factors must be borne in mind:

● The type of signal and the method of displaying the signal head (*e.g.* straight post, angled post, gantry etc)
● Assessment of the minimum reading time and the effect of interruptions present during that time
● The red aspect should be as near as possible to driver's eye level
● The centre of the light beam should generally be aligned towards a point 10ft (3m) above the left-hand running rail at 200 yards (180m) from the signal (*i.e.* where the AWS magnets are usually located)
● The desirability of providing banner or co-acting signals

Other factors to be borne in mind are:

● Where practicable the avoidance of sites on viaducts, steep gradients, in tunnels, across level crossings, or part train length beyond a platform

Above: Co-acting multiple-aspect colour-light signals at Platform 14 at Manchester Piccadilly station. The lower signal is provided for the benefit of drivers standing close to the signal. *Author*

- The position of neutral sections on overhead electrified lines and conductor-rail gaps on third-rail electrified lines, to avoid the risk of trains being brought to a stand on 'dead' sections
- The avoidance of environmental nuisance to lineside neighbours near signals at which trains are regularly stopped, caused by the noise of trains braking or accelerating, or the sound of engines idling or compressors working
- The possibility of vandalism to trains or signalling equipment
- The possibility of pilfering from stationary freight trains

Risk-assessment of signals

All signals that protect junctions have been risk-assessed using a tool known as the *signal-assessment tool*. The outcome is a numerical value that determines whether any further action needs to be considered to reduce the consequences if a SPAD occurs. Signals whose score is above a benchmark figure must be specially considered by an expert group to see what further measures, in addition to existing TPWS, could be provided. Such measures could include changes to signalling controls in the form of robust train protection.

Risk assessment is complementary to signal sighting. Risk assessment is focused on minimising the consequences of a SPAD should one occur, whereas the objective of signal sighting is to minimise the likelihood of a signal's being passed at Danger in the first place.

Platform starting signals

A number of serious accidents occurred in the past when drivers departed from a station and wrongly passed the platform starting signal when it was at Danger (known as a *start-against-signal SPAD* or SASSPAD). Protection against this risk is now most effectively provided by TPWS and to a lesser extent by the Driver's Reminder Appliance.

A variant of the SASSPAD is the *start-on-yellow SPAD* or SOYSPAD. This problem arises when a train starts from a platform starting signal displaying a single yellow aspect, which means that the next signal ahead at that time will be at Danger. In these circumstances, a driver must always remember that he may have to stop at the first signal, and control his speed accordingly. A SOYSPAD may occur if the driver forgets the aspect shown by the platform starting signal and continues to accelerate; by the time the next signal comes into view, the train may be going too fast to be able to stop in time and the signal may be protecting a junction. TPWS may not be an effective measure in these circumstances.

Good approach visibility of platform starting signals from the driver's position is essential if the likelihood of a SPAD is to be minimised. To provide it the stopping point is now typically 28 yards (25m) before the starting signal, where the length of the platform allows. For new signalling schemes, this may require platforms to be lengthened. Another measure that can help the driver is the provision of miniature repeating signals at cab height.

Before the introduction of TPWS, certain locations where there was a particularly high risk of collision if a signal was passed at Danger were provided with *SPAD indicators* and these were not removed when TPWS was fitted. A SPAD indicator is similar to a normal three-aspect colour-light signal and is located about 55 yards (50m) beyond the signal concerned.

SPAD indicators normally display no aspect, but when the signal to which they refer is passed at Danger they immediately display the following aspects to tell the driver that he has passed a signal at Danger: the top and bottom aspects flash red, and the centre aspect displays a steady red light. The driver must stop at once and tell the signaller what has happened. The driver must also stop his train and report to the signaller if he sees a SPAD indicator flashing for a signal on another line. This is a safety precaution in case his train is on a collision course with the other train.

A SPAD indicator may also have an AWS magnet positioned on its approach. It is suppressed for normal signalled movements, but gives an AWS warning when the SPAD indicator is triggered.

Driver's reminder appliance

The driver must depress the button of his Driver's Reminder Appliance (see Chapter 18) when stopped at any signal at Danger. When depressed the button illuminates red and prevents the traction power from being applied until the button has been pulled out. The driver must not reset the DRA until the signal has cleared.

Additionally the driver must set the DRA when he stops at a platform where there is no starting signal, in any of the following circumstances:

- When he has just passed a signal at Caution

- When he has been authorised to pass a signal at Danger
- When he has entered the platform under the authority of a position-light signal or a subsidiary signal

He must not reset the DRA until the 'Ready to start' signal is received. Some trains are fitted with an 'active DRA', which is applied automatically when a train passes a Caution signal.

As an additional safety measure, the guard must check (where practicable) that the platform starting signal has been cleared before he gives the 'Ready to start' signal to the driver. The same arrangement applies to a person in charge of a platform before he gives a handsignal to the guard to indicate that station work is complete or gives the 'Ready to start' signal to the driver of a driver-only train.

Where a *right-away indicator*, displaying the letters 'RA' when operated, is provided the indication is not displayed until the platform starting signal is cleared. This is an important safeguard against a mistake being made by the guard in giving the right-away signal with the starting signal at Danger.

The signaller's actions

If a train passes a signal at Danger without authority, the signaller must immediately arrange for the train to be stopped and take any other necessary emergency action. He must speak to the driver and ask a number of questions printed on a SPAD report form. Details must be given to Operations Control, and the signaller must not allow the train to proceed without its authority. If there is any doubt about the correct working of a signal, the signal must be treated as being defective.

SPAD alarms are provided in integrated electronic control centres to alert the signaller and give an immediate audible alarm and visual message when a signal is passed at Danger. The visual message displays the identification numbers of the signal and train concerned.

In many respects the principles of the Absolute Block double-line system apply to the working of single lines, but in addition to the normal dangers of working trains over a double line there is the extra hazard on single lines of the head-on collision caused by a train irregularly entering a section already occupied by a train coming the other way. To safeguard against this, the *Electric Token Block* system was devised, based on the principle that every train passing through a single-line section must carry a token, obtained from a *token instrument*, of which there is one at each end of each section. The instruments at each end of a section are electrically interlocked so that it is only possible for one token to be 'out' (*i.e.* in use) for the section at one and the same time. The token may take the form of a circular tablet, a few inches in diameter, or a metal key about 6 inches (150mm) long. It is placed in a leather pouch with a large loop handle to facilitate the handover from the signaller to the driver and vice versa. The token is withdrawn from the token instrument when the 'Is line clear?' bell signal is acknowledged, and is inserted in the instrument at the other end of the section when the train has passed through the section and the 'Train out of section' bell signal has been sent. Each instrument contains several tokens.

At a crossing loop on a single line, a train may be accepted from the signalbox in rear only if the loop line for which the facing points are set and on which the train will run is clear to the loop exit signal. When trains are approaching a crossing place from opposite directions, the home signals in both directions must be kept at Danger, until the train that is to enter the loop first has stopped, after which the home signal may be cleared to allow it to draw forward. When it has stopped again in the loop, the home signal may be cleared for the other train to enter the loop on the other side.

The tokenless-block system
In the *tokenless-block system* safety is provided by the sequential occupation and clearance of track circuits at both signalboxes, so that the signals cannot be cleared for a second train to

enter the section from either direction until the previous train is proved to have passed through the section. Tokens are not used, hence the name of the system.

The method of signalling is as follows.

1. Trains are accepted by placing an *acceptance switch* in the 'Accept' position. This is the usual position, depending on the expected movement of trains.
2. Before the dispatch of a train, the signaller must press the 'Offer' button, provided that the block indicator and the acceptance switch for that section are at 'Normal'. If the acceptance switch at the signalbox in advance is at 'Accept', the block indicators in both signalboxes will move to 'Train accepted', and the signaller in rear may then clear his signal and tell his colleague the description of the train. When the train occupies the track circuit ahead of the section signal, the block indicator will move to 'Train in section'. After the train has passed through the section, it registers its arrival by operating a treadle at the home signal; and after it has occupied and cleared the track circuit ahead of the home signal the signaller there must place the acceptance switch to 'Normal'.
3. When the train, complete with its tail lamp, arrives, the signaller must operate the 'Train arrived' button, which will restore the block indicators to 'Normal'. The acceptance switch must be maintained at 'Normal' until the train has passed the clearing point.

This description of the method of signalling is based on the installation on the Salisbury–Exeter line. The Scottish Region tokenless block functioned in a different way.

One-train working
This system is in widespread use on dead-end branch lines where the train service is so infrequent that it does not need more than one train to be on the branch at the same time.

There are two methods. In one, a token known as a *train staff* is provided, and the driver must not enter the branch line unless he is in possession of it. In the other, there is no train staff, and the clearance of the controlling signal is the only authority for the train to enter the branch. Safety in the latter case is achieved by the occupation and clearance of a track circuit, located at the entrance to the branch, on two occasions (*i.e.* when the train enters and when it returns). The controlling signal cannot be cleared for a second train until the first one is proved to have returned by the operation of the track circuits.

A train staff is provided at locations where there is someone, usually a signaller, who can act as its custodian and hand it over to the driver when necessary. The other method — the *tokenless* method — is used mainly on lines controlled from a remote signalbox, such as a power signalbox, where there is no one available at or near the branch entrance who can look after the train staff.

Above: The East Suffolk line RETB control centre in the signalbox at Saxmundham. *Brian Morrison*

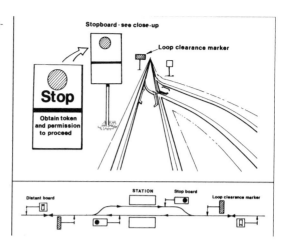

Right: Typical single-track branch line with passing loops worked under the Electronic Token Block system.

Above: RETB signals at Dovey Junction. *Author*

The 'no signaller' token system

The *'no signaller' token* system is one, used mainly on dead-end branch lines, which allows one train to follow another along a branch line as soon as the first is proved to have arrived at the far end of the branch. It is achieved by the use of tokens, and has a token instrument at each end of the branch line. The token instrument at the junction of the main line and the branch is operated by the signaller, who issues a token in the usual way to

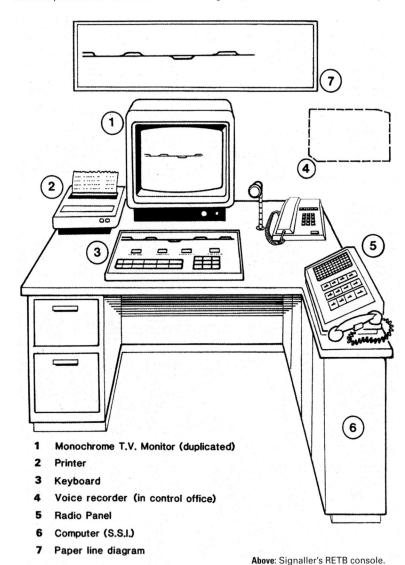

1 **Monochrome T.V. Monitor (duplicated)**
2 **Printer**
3 **Keyboard**
4 **Voice recorder (in control office)**
5 **Radio Panel**
6 **Computer (S.S.I.)**
7 **Paper line diagram**

Above: Signaller's RETB console.

a driver to proceed onto the branch line, provided that no other token is 'out'. When the train arrives at the far end of the branch, and is clear of an 'End of Single Line Section' noticeboard, the driver places the token in an instrument there, thus allowing another train to use the branch line, either by following him or by setting off in the opposite direction. It avoids the cost of having a signalbox and signaller at the branch end. The signaller controls the issue of tokens from the machine at the far end, by the use of a release.

Failures of equipment

With all these systems, provision must be made for train movements to continue safely, albeit at reduced speed, when the signalling equipment controlling the tokens is faulty, or a token is lost or damaged, or track circuits have failed. It is vital to ensure that only one train is in the single-line section at once, and this is done by introducing a system known as *working by pilotman*. In this system someone is appointed pilotman, who is responsible for the safety of the single line. He must personally authorise drivers to proceed and must travel through the single-line section with the driver when the next train requiring to pass through the single-line section will do so from the other end. On 'one train working' sections the pilotman must travel with every train.

The Radio Electronic Token Block (RETB) system

The *Radio Electronic Token Block* (RETB) system was born of the need to reduce the costs of working the long single lines to be found in northern Scotland, central Wales and elsewhere, in order to avoid having to close them down. It requires no intermediate signalboxes or signallers, nor does it require a vulnerable telegraph pole route, because all messages are sent by radio. It is based in theory on the well-tried and reliable electric token block system, but the 'token' is passed between signaller and driver electronically by radio, instead of physically by hand.

The whole line is controlled by one signaller, who has at his disposal an operating console containing a representation of the track under his control, together with electronic equipment and computers which look after safety. Each driver's cab is equipped with radio and an RETB instrument with two windows in which the electronic token displays its presence by showing the two ends of the section through which the driver is authorised to travel.

When the driver wishes to enter a single-line section he radios the signaller for permission. If the previous train in the same direction has passed through the section and cleared the next crossing loop, and if no train has been authorised to proceed through the section from the other end, the signaller issues an electronic token to the driver. To enable this to take place, the driver and the signaller must simultaneously press a button on their equipment; this procedure is known as a *handshake*. The driver will then confirm that he has received the token, because it will have appeared on the RETB instrument in his cab, and the signaller will verbally authorise him to proceed (this takes the place of the section signal). On entering the single-line section the driver reports to the signaller by radio as soon

Above: RETB hydro-pneumatic points. *D. C. Hall*

as his train has cleared the loop. This is important for two reasons: first, because as soon as the loop is clear, another train travelling in the same direction can be allowed to leave the loop in rear, and secondly, because if for any reason the driver had left the loop and entered the single-line section without authority (which is potentially very dangerous) the signaller would become aware of it and tell the driver to stop at once. He would also issue a similar instruction to the driver of any train coming through the single-line section in the opposite direction.

In order to keep costs down, the points at loops are not normally worked by the signaller (who is likely to be many miles away) but are hydro-pneumatically operated so that they always lie towards the same loop line. They are capable of being trailed through from the other loop line. In the facing direction a points indicator may be provided which displays a steady yellow light when the points are fitting correctly. When a train has entered a loop and is clear of the single-line section, the driver informs the signaller accordingly by radio. The two men will then simultaneously press the appropriate buttons on their equipment, and the electronic token will be returned to the signaller. The driver's RETB

instrument display will clear, and the token appear on the signaller's console display. If the section ahead is clear, the procedure for the issue of an electronic token for that section may then take place to enable the driver to proceed.

The signalbox computer ensures that tokens are issued in the correct sequence, keeps a record of all trains on the line, and prevents the signaller from authorising conflicting train movements.

The RETB system can be modified in several ways. For example, the loop points can be operated, detected and locked by radio command, to avoid the train having to pass through them at low speed; and transponders located in the track can detect the position of the train and announce it by radio to the signaller.

TPWS has been fitted to lines equipped with the RETB system, necessitating the provision of special equipment to suppress the train-stop sensors when an electronic token has been issued. This in turn necessitated the development of an indicator to advise drivers when the TPWS is suppressed, which consists of a blue light. When the TPWS is active, the indicator shows steady, but when it is suppressed the indicator flashes.

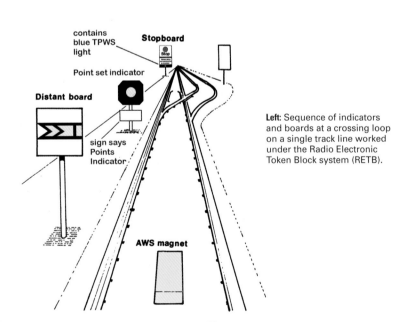

Left: Sequence of indicators and boards at a crossing loop on a single track line worked under the Radio Electronic Token Block system (RETB).

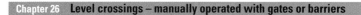

PART 6

Chapter 26 Level crossings – manually operated with gates or barriers

The following table lists the various types of manually operated level crossing, along with the number of each type in use on Network Rail in 2008:

Gates operated by a signaller or crossing-keeper on site	191
Barriers operated by a signaller or crossing-keeper on site	234
Barriers operated remotely by a signaller or crossing-keeper and supervised by CCTV	380

It should be noted that level crossing gates and barriers are not considered to be an obstruction so far as the acceptance of trains is concerned.

Gates operated by a signaller on site

These gates swing alternately across the road and the railway. Legally, they are required to be normally closed across the road, but the Office of Rail Regulation may authorise the gates at any particular level crossing to be normally closed across the railway, and this has been done at most level crossings because of the frequency of road traffic. The gates are interlocked with the railway signals in such a way that the signals cannot be cleared unless the gates are across the road. Once the signals have been cleared the gates cannot then be moved back across the railway. Where necessary, wicket gates may be provided, normally capable of being locked in the closed position by the signaller.

Above: Traditional gated level crossing at Elsenham, worked by a crossing keeper. *Author*

Above: A barrier-control console at Oakham level crossing. *D. C. Hall*

Where road traffic is heavy, and the signaller finds it difficult to swing his gates across the road because there are insufficient gaps in the traffic, road-traffic-light signals may be provided, which the signaller can switch to red to enable him to swing his gates. The gates are often operated by a large wheel in the signalbox, but in other cases are pushed across by hand.

Gates operated by a crossing-keeper on site

These gates are usually to be found in rural areas where neither road nor rail traffic is heavy. For historical reasons they are of many types. They may be operated by a crossing-keeper who lives in a cottage at the crossing, or they may be operated by non-resident crossing-keepers, working shifts, or by a combination of both, depending on the flow of road and rail traffic.

The gates may be of the signalbox type alternately closing the road and the railway, or they may be field gates that open away from the railway. The gates are normally pushed across by hand.

Protecting railway signals are provided at some, but not all, crossings of this type. In some cases both distant and stop signals are provided (normally semaphore); in other cases only distant signals are provided. Sometimes the signals are interlocked with the gates, and sometimes they are not.

There are various methods of informing the crossing-keeper whether he may open the gates to allow road traffic to cross. At some crossings duplicate block indicators are provided. Duplicate bells may be provided. At other crossings the crossing-keeper has to telephone a nearby signalbox to ask the signaller if road traffic may be allowed across.

Barriers operated by a signaller or crossing-keeper on site (MCBs)

Barriers operated by a signaller or crossing-keeper on site are known as *manually controlled crossings* or MCBs. Lifting barriers are normally installed as a modern replacement for gates, and are operated electrically. The barriers close the full width of the road at each side of the level crossing when lowered, but are normally kept in the raised position. They are interlocked with the protecting railway signals, and there are usually road traffic-light signals too.

When the operator wishes to lower the barriers he presses a button marked 'Lower' on his control console. The amber light on the road traffic signals shows for about 3 seconds, after which the red lights start to flash. After 4-8 seconds the nearside barriers start to descend, and when they are fully lowered the offside barriers descend. Before he can clear the railway signals, the operator must then check that the crossing is clear (i.e. that no vehicle or person is trapped on the crossing between the lowered barriers) and press a 'Crossing clear' button. Both the barrier lowering and raising sequences can be initiated automatically by trains through the operation of track circuits, but it is still necessary for the operator to check that the crossing is clear, and press the 'Crossing clear' button, before he can clear the railway signals. After the train has passed, all the barriers rise simultaneously.

Barriers operated remotely by a signaller or crossing-keeper and supervised by CCTV

The barrier equipment and method of control are similar to an MCB crossing, the only difference being that instead of the signaller checking visually that the crossing is clear he does so by means of a closed-circuit television (CCTV) camera mounted at the level crossing, which relays a picture to a screen in the signalbox. Audible and visual indications are provided at the signalbox to show if the main power supply fails, or if a barrier is dislodged (e.g. by high wind or a road vehicle running into it).

CCTV installations enable a signaller to control level crossings away from the signalbox, and enable crossing-keepers to control additional distant level crossings. One operator can control several crossings, and CCTV operation is widely used in power-signalbox areas. The railway signals are interlocked with the barriers.

Above: Barrier level crossing at Paignton, operated remotely by the signaller and monitored by CCTV. *Author*

The following table lists the various types of automatic level crossing, along with the number of each type in use on Network Rail in 2008:

Automatic half-barrier crossings (AHB)	452
Automatic barrier crossings, locally monitored (ABCL)	48
Automatic open crossings, locally monitored (AOCL)	120

ABCL crossings are a more recent development, hence the smaller number. Many were converted from the now obsolete automatic crossings, remotely monitored (AOCR), of which there remains only one, at Rosarie, between Keith and Elgin

Automatic half-barrier crossings (AHBs)

Automatic half-barrier crossings, first introduced on British Railways in 1961, have three objectives:

1. To avoid the staffing costs of ordinary level crossings
2. To reduce the delays caused to road traffic by conventional gated level crossings or those with manually controlled barriers
3. To improve safety at level crossings, by eliminating the human element

So far as these three objectives are concerned, AHBs are introduced only where their costs are more than outweighed by the saving in staff costs. They considerably reduce delays to road traffic because they are not interlocked with railway signals, so that the crossing does not need to be closed for such a long period. At a staffed crossing, the road has to be closed and the railway signals cleared before the driver of an approaching train has come within sight of the distant signal. At AHBs the railway signals act independently of the operation of the level crossing; the nearest railway signals may be green while road traffic is passing over the crossing. As far as safety is concerned, they eliminate only the element of human error amongst railway staff; they do not eliminate the careless or reckless motorist who ignores the red flashing lights and deliberately zig-zags around the barriers, occasionally at the cost of his life.

The barriers are operated by an approaching train occupying a particular track circuit, reinforced by a treadle at the running-on end (*i.e.* the end remote from the crossing) to guard against unreliable operation of the track circuit

Above: Automatic half-barrier level crossing at Swainsthorpe. *Author*

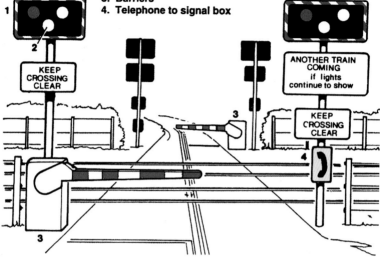

Key:
1. Twin flashing red lights
2. Single amber light
3. Barriers
4. Telephone to signal box

KEEP CROSSING CLEAR

ANOTHER TRAIN COMING
if lights continue to show

KEEP CROSSING CLEAR

Drivers of
LARGE or SLOW VEHICLES
must phone
and get permission
to cross

LARGE means over
61'-6" (18.75m) long or
9'-6" (2.9m) wide or
44 tonnes total weight
SLOW means 5 mph or less

PARK HERE
AND USE
PHONE AT
CROSSING

Above: An automatic half-barrier level crossing, showing the layout, road-traffic signals etc.

Left: Warning notices on the approach to Black Dyke AHB crossing (Arnside). *Author*

by lightweight rail vehicles, and this triggers the following sequence of events.

1. An amber light shows for about 3 seconds.
2. Twin red lights start to flash alternately.
3. After 4-6 seconds the barriers start to lower. The barrier lowering operation takes between 6 and 10 seconds.
4. An audible warning sounds during the whole of this period.
5. Not less than 27 seconds after the amber lights first show, the train passes over the crossing.
6. The barriers rise as soon as the train has cleared the crossing, unless another train is approaching, in which case they remain down unless at least 10 seconds can elapse, after the barriers have begun to rise, before the operating cycle starts again for the next train.

The equipment at the crossing is monitored from a control point (usually a signalbox) and emergency telephones are provided for the public to speak to the control point.

AHBs may be provided only where the following conditions apply:

1. The maximum speed of trains does not exceed 100mph (160km/h).
2. There are no more than two running lines (though there may be two sidings as well).
3. The road on the approaches to the crossing is wide enough to enable vehicles to pass safely (*i.e.* without blocking back on to the crossing while waiting to pass).
4. There are no bumps or hollows on the road that might cause a low vehicle to ground on the crossing (known as the *vertical profile*).
5. The road layout and the traffic conditions are such that there is no significant risk of road vehicles' blocking back and obstructing the railway (*e.g.* there are no road junctions near by, and the road traffic does not experience frequent hold-ups).

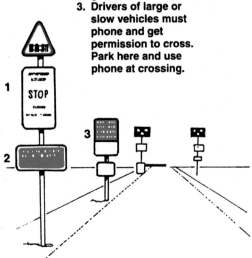

Key:
1. **Automatic barriers stop when lights show**
2. **Drivers of large or slow vehicles phone before crossing**
3. **Drivers of large or slow vehicles must phone and get permission to cross. Park here and use phone at crossing.**

Right: Road users advance warning of an AHB crossing.

Right: Speed restriction board for trains approaching an AHB level crossing in the wrong direction.

Equipment is provided at the level crossing to allow the lights and barriers to be locally controlled on site in circumstances such as:

1. Failure of equipment
2. Repairs to the equipment
3. Work on the track
4. Roadworks near the crossing that might cause traffic to block back.

When the crossing is being controlled locally, the signaller must warn the driver of each train to approach the crossing cautiously and not pass over it unless authorised by a green flag or lamp being displayed by the attendant.

Some AHB crossings are adapted to allow wrong-direction movements to operate the barrier equipment in the normal way. Such crossings are known as *AHB-X level crossings*, and the train speed must not exceed that shown on a *wrong direction speed restriction board*, which has black numerals prefixed by the letter X on a white background and is normally positioned on the right-hand side of the line.

When barriers fail in the lowered position, or the red road traffic signals continue to flash during a failure of equipment at an automatic open crossing, no railway employee may authorise road users to disregard the road traffic signals. Only a police officer in uniform may do this. The police officer will contact the signaller by using the level crossing telephone, and must not be given authority to allow road traffic to cross until protecting signals have been placed to Danger. After this has been done, trains must not be allowed to approach the crossing until the police officer has given an assurance that road traffic has been stopped.

Automatic barrier crossings, locally monitored (ABCL)

Automatic open crossings, locally monitored (AOCL)
These types of crossing are installed where the nature of the train service allows speeds to be reduced on the approach to the crossing to a level

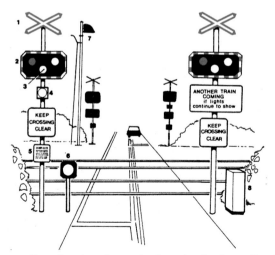

Key:
1. **Crossing sign**
2. **Twin flashing red lights**
3. **Single amber light**
4. **Yodalarm unit**
5. **Sign showing local Network Rail telephone numbers**
6. **Red flashing signal 'another train coming'**
7. **Floodlight angled to crossing**
8. **Local contol unit**

Above: An automatic open level crossing, locally monitored (AOCL), showing the layout, road-traffic signals, signs etc.

at which the train driver can check: first, that the road traffic signals are flashing (and the barriers at ABCLs are lowered), secondly, that the crossing is not obstructed by a stationary or very slow moving road vehicle, and, thirdly, that the train can stop before reaching the crossing in the event of failure or obstruction. ABCLs and AOCLs are cheaper to install than AHBs because the monitoring of operation is done locally by the train driver, instead of remotely (using expensive cable) by the signaller. Also, the road requirements at AOCLs are not so stringent as they are at AHB crossings. There are many level crossings on secondary lines, especially those operated on only two shifts, where an AHB crossing would be too expensive, but where an economic case can be made for the installation of locally monitored level crossing equipment.

There are certain restrictions on the provision of AOCL crossings, depending on the *traffic moment*, whereas the ABCL crossing has no such traffic restrictions; but the ABCL crossing must satisfy some additional road conditions. Traffic moment denotes the combination of trains and road vehicles in any hour; for example 15 road vehicles and 2 trains an hour would represent a traffic moment of 30.

The road-traffic signals (and the half barriers at ABCLs) are operated automatically by the occupation of track circuits by approaching trains, but in addition treadles are provided at the strike-in point, owing to problems with the unreliability of track-circuit operation by lightweight vehicles. A white flashing light, adjacent to the crossing and facing the train driver, indicates that the road traffic signals are operating correctly. A red light flashes when the white light is not flashing.

The train driver is warned that he is approaching a locally monitored crossing by a board bearing a black St George's cross on a white background. He must then reduce his speed (if necessary) so that he can pass a speed restriction board at the appropriate speed. On passing the speed restriction board (with black numerals and a black St Andrew's cross on a white background), he must check that the crossing is clear and that the white light is flashing, and then proceed to the crossing at the speed shown on the speed restriction board, which is known as the *crossing speed*. The maximum crossing speed allowed is 56mph (90km/h).

If the white light adjacent to the crossing is not flashing, or if the crossing cannot be seen to be clear, and in other specified circumstances, the driver must stop short of the crossing and not proceed over it until he is sure it is safe to do so. The horn must be sounded continuously until the front of the train is on the crossing. During darkness, however, a train must not pass over an AOCL crossing when the road traffic signals have failed unless it is a passenger or ECS train with the lights on, or unless other safety arrangements have been made.

Above: Automatic open crossing, locally monitored (AOCL) at Dolau, on the Central Wales line. Some crossings display minor variations. *Author*

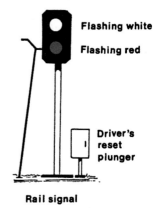

Flashing white

Flashing red

Driver's reset plunger

Rail signal

Above: Signal for train driver on the approach to an automatic open crossing.

Above: Lineside signs warning the train driver that he is approaching an AOCL warning board (*top*) and an AOCL speed-restriction board (*above*).

The speed restriction board is located near the point at which the operating cycle for the crossing begins. The operating cycle is as follows:

1. An amber light shows for 3 seconds
2. The twin red road traffic signals start to flash alternately
3. The train arrives at the crossing not less than 27 seconds after the amber light first shows

The crossing speed is therefore determined by the speed necessary to give at least 27 seconds' warning from the point at which the crossing comes into the driver's view, so that he can stop safely before reaching the crossing if it is seen to be obstructed. A sharply curved approach, where a crossing does not come into view until the train is fairly close to it, therefore needs a lower crossing speed than one that comes into clear view from a greater distance. The crossing speed board must not be more than 660 yards

(600m) from the flashing rail signals at the crossing.

Some speed restriction boards carry two figures. The bottom figure (the higher speed) applies to passenger trains, and the top figure (the lower speed) applies to all other trains.

Level crossings are often situated at or near the ends of station platforms. In such cases a speed restriction board is not provided, but there is a 'STOP' board near the crossing. When the train is ready to restart, a plunger is pressed, which causes the road traffic signals to flash. The driver must check before starting and passing the 'STOP' board that the crossing is clear and that the white light is flashing. He must then sound the horn. At some places the flashing of the lights is caused automatically, instead of manually by plunger.

An audible warning is sounded at the crossing as a train approaches. If the lights continue to flash after the train has passed over the crossing the audible warning will change, and a special flashing light will illuminate the words 'Another train coming'. There are no telephones, but a plate gives the telephone number of a suitable railway office and also the name of the crossing.

Equipment is provided at some crossings to enable wrong-direction movements to be made in the normal way, the arrangements being similar to those at AHB-X crossings (see p97). These crossings are known as *ABCL-X* and *AOCL-X* crossings.

Open crossings

Open level crossings are to be found on quiet single lines, where the traffic moment (see p98) is not more than 30 in any hour. The raffic moment denotes the combination of trains and road vehicles; for example 15 road vehicles and two trains an hour would represent a traffic moment of 30. The crossings are non-automatic, there are no gates or barriers, and there are no flashing red road-traffic signals. Road signs require road users to give way to trains, and satisfactory visibility of approaching trains is necessary. Trains either approach the crossing at 10mph (15km/h) or stop at a 'STOP' board 28 yards (25m) from it. They must stop if the road users' view of approaching trains is inadequate (or *vice versa*). There are no telephones. There were 51 of these crossings on Network Rail in 2008.

On the railway, an *advance warning board* is provided at braking distance to enable trains to reduce speed to 10mph, or stop. The board carries a black St George's cross on a white background. A speed restriction/whistle board is provided at a point from which the driver has a clear view of the crossing and from which he can stop the train short of the crossing if necessary.

Level crossings with gates or barriers operated by the road user or a member of the train crew

Level crossings with gates or barriers operated by the road user or a member of the train crew fall into three categories (figures for 2008):

1. Crossings equipped with miniature warning lights (88)
2. Crossings equipped with a telephone (1,624)
3. Crossings with no equipment (980)

Almost all the level crossings we have considered in previous chapters have been on public roads, but the great majority of those that are dealt with in this chapter are private, and the public have no right to use them with a road vehicle, although there are footpath or bridleway rights at some. Private crossings are of two types: *occupation* level crossings and *accommodation* level crossings.

Above: Private road crossing at Moulinearn (Pitlochry) with barriers and miniature warning lights. Such crossings are normally provided with gates. *Author*

Occupation level crossings

These concern private roads which existed before the railway was built. The road may have served only one farm, or it may have served several farms and/or cottages. When the railway was built, the tracks were laid across the private road, creating an occupation crossing. In addition to those who have a right to use the crossing by virtue of residence, others who have business there may also use the crossing, such as delivery workers and tradespeople.

Accommodation level crossings

When the railway line was built it often ran through a piece of land in single ownership, dividing it into two. In order to provide access from one part of the divided land to the other it was necessary to construct accommodation bridges and level crossings, which frequently merely give access from a field at one side of the railway to another field at the other side. Many of these

Above: Warning sign at a private road level crossing that is not equipped with miniature warning lights. *Author*

Above: The signs normally provided at private road level crossings, normally of the 'occupation' type. *Author*

crossings, known colloquially as *sleeping dogs*, have fallen into disuse over the years, but still exist legally and are not included in the figures above.

The gates at occupation and accommodation crossings are almost always of the field type, which open away from the railway, and normally bear a notice requiring the user to shut and fasten the gates after use, with a penalty for failure to do so.

A few accommodation crossings have barriers, operated by the road user, which are raised by the operation of a pump handle. The user must lower the barriers after crossing.

Crossings equipped with miniature warning lights

These crossings have small red and green lights, operated by approaching trains, for the guidance of road users, and are therefore sometimes referred to as MWL crossings. Detailed instructions as to the use of the crossing are displayed on noticeboards at the crossing. The green light shows continuously until a train running at maximum line speed is about 40 seconds away, when it will be extinguished and the red light will show. If no light shows the noticeboard will warn the user to beware or to telephone the signaller, if a telephone is provided. Such a telephone may be provided if, for example, heavy farm plant or cattle are regularly taken over the crossing, or if the crossing is a public one.

Crossings where a telephone is provided

At private level crossings the road user is responsible for his own safety and must satisfy himself that it is safe to cross before doing so. Where the sighting distance of trains from the crossing is inadequate, or herds of animals or heavy machinery are regularly taken over, a telephone to a signalbox may be provided so that the user can ask the signaller if the crossing may be used. On each occasion the signaller must find out what is to be taken over the crossing; and if there is sufficient time for that movement to take place before the next train, the user must be so informed. If there is insufficient time he must tell the user to wait and telephone again. All calls are recorded by the signaller. The gates at private level crossings need not be locked.

It should be noted that there are a few public level crossings which, for historical reasons, do not conform to the principles set out in Part 6.

Public-footpath and bridleway crossings

In 2008 there were 2,483 footpath and bridleway crossings on Network Rail. They are protected by stiles (footpath crossings only) or outward-opening wicket gates on each side of the railway, and crossing users must exercise sufficient vigilance to cross safely. 'Stop, look, listen' and 'Beware of trains' notices are provided at each side.

Safety depends on users' being able to see approaching trains in sufficient time to be able to cross safely. Where this is not the case, 'Whistle' boards may be provided not more than 440 yards (400m) from the crossing, or where pedestrian use is heavy, miniature warning lights may be provided. Telephones may be provided at bridleway crossings.

Developments in level crossings

New technology is increasingly being applied to improve the safety of level crossings, including:

1. The greater use of 'predictors' to ensure that road users at automatic crossings have a constant warning time irrespective of the approach speed of a train. This should reduce temptation amongst road users to ignore the traffic-light signals.
2. The planned installation of automatic full-barrier level crossings combined with obstacle detection using radar to ascertain whether anything is trapped between the lowered barriers.
3. Low-cost warning systems based on warning lights and/or audible warnings for user-worked (occupation and accommodation) crossings.
4. The use of sophisticated risk assessment techniques to measure the risk at level crossings so that improvements can be targeted first at those that present the highest risk.

PART 7

Hot-axlebox detectors are provided on main lines about every 20-25 miles (32-40km), especially where there are no lineside signalboxes, to check whether there are any overheated axle bearings in passing trains. If not detected an overheated bearing could lead to a train's derailment or cause a fire. Signallers in lineside signalboxes are expected to look out for signs of hot axleboxes on passing trains, and have the trains stopped if necessary. Signallers can recognise a hot axlebox in a number of ways — by the smell of overheated material, by the sight of smoke or flames or by abnormal noises.

In the absence of a lineside signaller, hot axleboxes are detected by equipment located on the track. The hot axlebox detector (HABD) scans each axlebox passing over it for infra-red radiation which is emitted at normal and hot axle bearing temperatures. An alarm is sounded in the monitoring signalbox if a hot axle bearing is detected.

If the alarm sounds in the signalbox, the signaller will put the signals to Danger to stop the train. He will also stop trains on adjoining lines until the train with the hot axlebox has stopped and the driver has assured him that no other lines are affected (by a derailed vehicle, for example). As soon as the signaller has placed the signals to Danger, he must contact Operations Control to see whether the vehicle concerned is conveying dangerous goods.

When the driver reports to the signaller (normally by telephone), the signaller must tell him the axle number, counting from the front of the train (including the locomotive), and whether the hot axlebox is on the left- or right-hand side (the signalbox equipment displays these details). The driver must then examine the axlebox concerned for evidence of overheating, if necessary by feeling

Above: A typical hot-axlebox detector. *Author*

it or by using a temperature-indicating crayon known as a Tempilstik, and report his findings to the signaller.

If the axlebox is obviously hot, but the vehicle concerned is safe to be moved, it must be detached in a nominated siding (speed not to exceed 10mph (16km/h) on plain line and 5mph (8km/h) over points and crossings). If it is a passenger coach, the passengers should be moved out of the vehicle before it is detached. The signaller must stop trains on adjoining lines before authorising the driver to make the movement.

If no defect can be found, the train may proceed normally, but a further examination must be carried out within 50 miles (80km) by either a rolling stock technician or the driver, unless the train passes over a hot axlebox detector in working order without activating the alarm. If further examination reveals that there is nothing wrong, the train may resume its normal journey. If, however, the second detector sounds an alarm and the train has to be moved, its speed must not exceed 20mph (32km/h).

These instructions do not apply to steam locomotives in steam, which by their very nature are liable to cause false alarms.

The instructions to drivers and signallers are contained in Rule Book Module TW5, 'Preparation and movement of trains. Defective or isolated vehicles and on-train equipment', and are lengthy and complex. There are other systems such as hot axlebox detection built into vehicles and detection of hot brakes ('dragging' brakes).

Wheel-impact-load detectors (developed by AEA Technology Rail and known by the brand name WheelChex) are installed on the network to measure the impact loads of each wheel of a train and to measure whether these loads are outside acceptable limits, for example because of damage such as wheel flats or an overloaded vehicle. These conditions if not detected could cause damage to the track or increase the risk of derailment.

If an unacceptable wheel load is measured by the system, an alarm sounds in the local Operations Control, and a controller will then contact the appropriate signaller so that the train can be stopped for examination by the driver. Depending on the outcome, the train may be terminated or allowed to proceed forward at reduced speed.

All Network Rail's running lines are engineered and maintained for trains to run at specific speeds, and these are the maximum permissible speeds for the route concerned. They are published in a document known as the *Sectional Appendix*. These speeds, known as *line speeds*, are not constant throughout the route, but vary over different sections. The maximum permissible speed is indicated at the lineside by retroreflective circular signs with black numerals and a red border. (The older version of the sign consisting of yellow cut-out numerals can also still be seen.)

At certain places on the route, speed has to be reduced below the normal line speed owing for example to sharp curvature or the complexity of track layout. These reductions of speed are known as *permanent speed restrictions* (PSRs).

To assist the driver when he is approaching a location at which he needs to reduce speed (which may be either a section with a lower line speed, or a permanent speed restriction), an advance warning sign, known as a *warning indicator*, may be provided, sufficiently far back to allow the driver time to reduce speed to the required level. The warning indicator takes the form of a reflective triangular sign with black numerals and a yellow border. In addition, a permanent AWS magnet may be provided on the approach side of the sign, so that an audible warning is given in the driving cab, together with a TPWS overspeed sensor located between 440 and 660 yards (400-600m) before the commencement of the speed restriction.

The brakes are applied automatically if the driver does not acknowledge the warning, or has not reduced the train's speed to less than the speed setting of the TPWS. Warning indicators are provided where the approach speed is 60mph (97km/h) or more and the reduction of speed is one-third or more of the approach speed, for example:

Approach speed	Speed reduced to or below
125mph (201km/h)	85mph (137km/h)
100mph (161km/h)	65mph (105km/h)
80mph (129km/h)	50mph (80km/h)
60mph (97km/h)	35mph (56km/h)

The approach speed is considered to be the maximum permissible speed on the immediate approach to the restriction, but a lower speed may be assumed in certain circumstances.

Where there is a 'cascade' of speed restrictions (two or more within 2 miles), none of which may individually justify a warning indicator, but where there is a total speed reduction of more than one-third between the approach speed to the first restriction and the last in the cascade, a warning indicator is provided for the PSR that takes the total reduction in speed to more than one-third.

Where the warning indicator and/or permissible speed indicator applies to a diverging line, it carries an arrow, pointing left or right as appropriate. Where differential speeds apply, the warning indicator and the permissible-speed indicator show two speeds, one above the other. The bottom figure (the higher speed) applies only to passenger trains (loaded or empty), postal and parcels trains and light engines. The top figure (the lower speed) applies to all other trains.

Where the indicators show letters above the numerals the meaning is as follows:

HST new-generation diesel multiple-units (except Class 185), Class 220, 221 and 222 trains, Class 91 locomotives with Mk 4 coaches and driving van trailers, Class 253 and 254 High Speed Trains, Class 373 Eurostar trains and Class 390 'Pendolino' trains

MU Multiple-unit trains (except Class 185)

DMU Diesel multiple-unit trains (except Class 185)

EMU Electric multiple-unit trains

SP Classes 150-159 ('Sprinter'-type trains), Classes 165 and 166 and Classes 168, 170 and 171 ('Turbostars')

CS Class 67 locomotives

Above: Permanent speed-restriction signs.

3. Commencement sign

1. Warning indicator

2. Restriction on diverging line at a junction

Braking distance

AWS magnet

Where both HST and SP speeds apply at a location, trains of Classes 168, 170 and 171 are permitted to run at the higher of two speeds.

EPS signs show the permissible speeds for tilting trains (Classes 221, in tilting mode, and 390). The figure on the sign denotes the maximum enhanced permissible speed (EPS) for the section of line ahead and above the figure are the letters 'EPS'. In some cases, a differential enhanced permissible speed applies where the bottom figure (the higher speed) applies where the bottom figure (the higher speed) applies to Class 390 trains and the top figure (the lower speed) applies to Class 221 trains in tilting mode. Warning indicators replicate the information provided on the EPS signs.

Complications may arise where reductions of speed are necessary for two or more separate but adjoining permanent speed restrictions, where the warning board for the second restriction would otherwise precede the commencement sign for the first one. In such cases special arrangements may apply.

The location of the warning indicator is based on the distance needed to reduce speed to the required level from the maximum permitted approach speed, based on braking curves. The distance may be extended to ensure that the associated AWS magnet is at least 4 seconds away from any other magnet.

The arrangements for PSRs are described in Rule Book Module SP Part A, 'Permissible speeds and enhanced permissible speeds'.

Temporary speed restrictions (TSRs) are imposed where the track is not in a fit condition for trains to run on at the normal permissible speed, usually pending or following maintenance or renewals. The driver is informed of such restrictions in a number of ways:

1. By an entry in the *weekly operating notice* (WON) issued to all drivers, which contains a section listing all TSRs, route by route, for the area concerned.
2. By a notice in a special *late notice case* at the depot where the driver signs on duty. Drivers are required to read such notices every time they sign on duty.
3. By signs erected at the lineside, supplemented by an AWS permanent magnet.

The lineside signs are as follows:

1. A warning board, positioned on the left-hand side of the line at braking distance from the start of the TSR, and denoting the speed limit of the TSR. If it is a TSR beyond a diverging junction, the warning board will include a directional arrow, called a *directional indicator*. Differential speed restrictions may apply, in which case the bottom figure (the higher speed) applies only to passenger trains (loaded or empty), to postal and parcels trains and to light engines. The top figure (the lower speed) applies to all other trains.
2. A speed indicator at the start of the restriction, showing the permitted speed.
3. A termination indicator at the end of the restriction.

Where the normal position of a warning board falls on the approach side of a passenger station, a siding connection or a dead-end platform line, and the speed indicator is more than 330 yards (300m) ahead of that location, a *repeating warning board* is provided at the far end of the platform (or other appropriate location) as a reminder to the driver. The repeating warning board is a reflective sign with a horizontal yellow bar including two white discs, and with the letter 'R' above the bar.

The warning board, speed indicator and termination indicator are also reflective. The warning board consists of a horizontal yellow bar

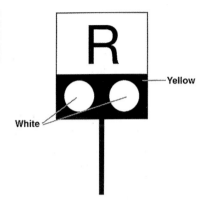

Above: Reflectorised repeating warning board at platform departure end.

containing two discs with the TSR value on a sign above the horizontal bar.

A portable AWS permanent magnet is placed in the 'four-foot' (between the rails) 200 yards (183m) on the approach side of the warning board; but where the appropriate location for the magnet falls near to a signal or its AWS magnets, it may be more convenient for the warning board to be placed at the signal, and for the signal magnet to be adjusted so that only a warning indication can be given, irrespective of the aspect shown by the signal.

Special arrangements regarding the location of warning boards etc apply where there are two adjacent TSRs.

A TSR may be withdrawn or eased earlier than is shown in the weekly operating notice, in which case the warning board and speed indicator will be altered to show the higher speed. If a TSR shown in the weekly operating notice is not imposed, the warning board etc must be erected unless a special notice cancelling the TSR has been issued at least 24 hours before the time when it was due to start. The warning board and speed indicator must be altered to show a 'SPATE' ('speed previously advised terminated early') indication (see drawing below).

If a TSR is withdrawn earlier than shown, or is not imposed, the speed indication in both the warning board and the speed indicator may be replaced by a SPATE indicator. Where there are TSRs on both routes at a diverging junction and the correct positions of both warning boards fall on the approach side of the junction, the second warning board must be positioned at least 50 yards (45m) beyond the first. The second warning board does not have an AWS magnet.

The driver must not resume normal speed until he is sure that the whole of the train has passed clear of the TSR.

A missing warning board etc must be dealt with as follows:

1. Warning board or speed indicator missing, in the wrong place or more restrictive than previously published in the weekly operating notice: the driver must tell the signaller at once, stopping his train specially if necessary. The signaller must warn all other drivers about it and tell Operations Control.
2. Warning board, a speed or termination indicator becoming difficult to see: the driver must tell the signaller at the first convenient opportunity. The signaller must inform Operations Control.

If a TSR does not finish on time it must be dealt with as an emergency speed restriction. Rule Book Module SP Part B, 'Temporary speed restrictions', is very comprehensive on this subject, and includes 10 coloured diagrams illustrating the various permutations regarding the placing of boards, indicators and permanent magnets.

Emergency temporary speed restrictions (ESRs)

When it is necessary to impose an ESR without notice to drivers, special steps must be taken to ensure that drivers are aware of it and do not take

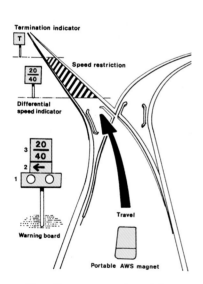

Above: Temporary speed-restriction signs —
(1) warning board,
(2) applicable to the diverging route, and
(3) differential speed indicator.

Speed indicator replaced by 'Spate' indication

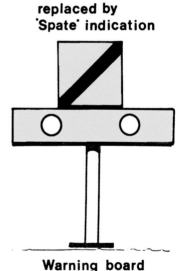

Warning board

Above: A SPATE indicator denotes that a restriction has been withdrawn or has not been imposed.

their trains over the ESR at more than the appropriate speed. The signaller must be told at once, and equipment must be provided without delay if the restriction is to continue for more than a short time. A *special notice* must be issued if an ESR is to continue for more than a short time.

The sequence of events after the need to impose an ESR has come to light is as follows:

1. If possible, trains should be diverted to another line or route until the equipment has been provided.
2. If it is necessary for trains to pass over the ESR before equipment is in position the signaller must stop all trains on the line affected and explain the situation to the driver, ensuring that he correctly understands exactly where the ESR is, and the speed over it, which must not exceed 20mph (32km/h). The train may then be allowed to proceed.
3. A warning board, portable AWS magnet, speed indicator and termination indicator must be erected under the same arrangement as for a TSR.
4. An emergency indicator, consisting of a black and yellow chequered board and two brilliant white flashing lights mounted vertically, must be erected 200 yards (183m) on the approach side of the warning board, together with a portable AWS magnet 200 yards before the emergency indicator. If the warning board is located less than ¼ mile

(400m) beyond a fixed signal equipped with AWS, the emergency indicator must be erected at the signal, and the AWS electromagnet must be disconnected so that a driver receives a warning irrespective of the aspect being displayed at the signal. In such circumstances an additional portable magnet is not required.

The emergency indicator must remain in position until details of the ESR are shown in the weekly operating notice or the restriction is withdrawn. The emergency indicator lights must be lit at all times. If it fails, the driver must tell the signaller at once, stopping specially if necessary. The signaller must inform all drivers affected and arrange for the emergency indicator to be repaired or replaced.

If a blanket emergency speed restriction has to be applied — for example, because of adverse weather affecting the infrastructure — this is done by Operations Control, which advises signallers and train operating companies; emergency indicators and other associated track equipment are not provided.

A TSR that has a lower speed than that shown in the weekly notice, or applies at a different time, must be treated as an ESR.

The arrangements described in this chapter are set out in Rule Book Module SP Part C, 'Emergency speed restriction'.

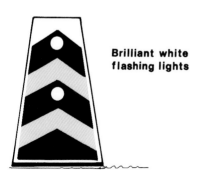

Brilliant white flashing lights

Emergency indicator

Below: Emergency indicator for an emergency speed restriction ahead.

PART 8

Chapter 32 Train-radio system

At present there are two quite distinct train-radio systems in use on Britain's railways. One is *Cab Secure Radio* (CSR); the other is the *National Radio Network* (NRN). Both are being replaced by a new system, GSM-R (Global System for Mobile Communications — Railway).

Cab Secure Radio (CSR)

Cab Secure Radio was designed in the late 1970s to be installed in trains that were to be operated without guards — now known as *driver-only operation* (DOO) — because the provision of this type of radio system was one of the safety requirements agreed by the British Railways Board and HM Railway Inspectorate for the operation of suburban passenger trains without guards. It is now used more widely and forms the normal method of communication between driver and signaller.

The other main requirements are that the line must be equipped with continuous train-detection equipment and multiple-aspect colour-light signalling. For technical reasons the line must be

Radio Area Boundary Signal - Cab Secure Radio

Similar Sign for the National Rail Network with the letters NRN

Above: Sign indicating the radio-area boundary in a Cab Secure Radio area.

controlled by a signalbox equipped with modern train-describer equipment.

The boundaries between radio areas are indicated by lineside signs. When a train passes one of these signs the radio channel in use on the train is changed automatically.

Method of operation

When a train enters traffic or changes its train-description number the driver must send to a management processor in the controlling signalbox a data message that states the number of the signal at which the train is standing. The call number of the train's radio equipment (known as the *train stock number*) is automatically included in this message, so that the call number can automatically be correlated with the train-description number. This is necessary because the signaller does not know the call number of any particular train, and must use the train-description number to obtain radio communication with a driver. Similarly, when the driver wishes to speak to the signaller, he operates his radio to send a call signal to the signalbox, which is indicated to the signaller by the train-description number of that train appearing on a visual-display unit (VDU). Incoming calls are queued, but if a driver makes an emergency call, this is shown separately on the VDU, and the signaller must respond urgently. The driver cannot speak until the signaller opens the communication channel, but the signaller can initiate a call to a driver at any time. All calls are recorded.

The signaller can ascertain at once from his signalling control panel where the train is, by looking for the train-description number. Strict radio procedures are followed, although the system is designed to ensure that the signaller knows which driver he is speaking to. The radio messages between the signaller and a driver cannot be overheard by other drivers, so there is no danger of another driver's acting on an instruction from the signaller that is not meant for him; but the signaller can, if he wishes, broadcast a general message to all drivers in a particular area. The signaller can also speak to the passengers in a train over the train's public-address system.

The National Radio Network (NRN)

The National Radio Network (NRN) was first installed c1980, to provide radio communication between the radio control office and personnel out on the line and facilitate the more efficient management of engineers' possessions of the line. It also enabled electrification telephones on AC overhead electric lines to be removed. The system took a long time to reach its full potential, owing to the unreliability of the software and inadequate radio coverage, but enough base stations have now been provided to give almost complete coverage of the railway system. NRN also provides radio communication with the railway extension trunk dialling (ETD) telephone system.

The advantages of having radio communication with trains are obvious, but the high cost of Cab Secure Radio and the technical difficulties of installing it nationwide meant that thoughts turned to the possibility of using or adapting the National Radio Network for the purpose, and this was done.

Calls from driving cabs my be made only in the following circumstances:

● When a train has failed or has a defect and needs assistance or technical examination, or the driver needs technical advice
● When the Rules require the driver to report to the signaller his presence at a signal but the telephone has failed, or there is a sign indicating limited safety clearance; at such signals a diamond sign bears the telephone number for the controlling signalbox
● When it is necessary to give or ask for information about train working, delays, connectional arrangements etc
● During engineering work, when agreed

If the signaller is unable to call the driver direct, he must arrange, via a third party, for the driver to call him.

NRN is not classed as a secure radio system, since there is no correlation between the train's radio call number and the train-description number. The signaller is not normally aware of the radio call number of a particular train, and the radio traffic is normally initiated by drivers.

Boundaries between NRN radio zones are indicated by a lineside sign, and the driver must reset the radio when passing one of these signs.

Use of radio by signaller in an emergency

When the Train Signalling Regulations require the signaller to stop a train in an emergency, the signaller must use radio if it may enable the train to be stopped more quickly. He must also carry out the regulation concerned.

The emergency-call procedure

A driver can use his train radio to obtain access to the railway telephone network and can make an emergency call by pressing a red button, which connects him immediately with an Operations Control office. The control office receiving the emergency call can broadcast a message to all trains within a particular base station's radio coverage area, which will be heard over the loudspeaker in driving cabs. The opportunity for avoiding mishap, or further mishap, is thus enhanced.

The emergency-call procedure must only be used when it is necessary for other trains to be stopped or cautioned owing to an accident or obstruction or other exceptional incident, or when the emergency services are needed.

If the driver has used the emergency-call procedure and is unable to speak directly to the signaller but only to a third party, he must:

1. Stop his train at once and tell the signaller, using a signalpost telephone
2. Carry out any protection of the line which is necessary

Making an emergency call cuts off all normal calls and connects the caller immediately with Operations Control.

Global System for Mobile Communications — Railways (GSM-R)

By the early 1990s it had become clear that NRN and CSR were technically obsolescent. Comparable systems elsewhere in Europe were also in need of replacement, so the opportunity was taken to develop a new specification that would be mandatory throughout the European Union. This led to a decision to adopt the GSM system, which would not only be a replacement for both NRN and CSR but also act as the bearer for the new European Train Control System (ETCS).

One of the main constituents of the GSM-R system is the *base transmitting station* (BTS). Base transmitting stations are spaced around 5-6km apart and provide the transmitter/receiver points at the lineside. The BTS consists of a radio station, a power supply and a tower or mast supporting the aerials. Eventually there are likely to be around 3,000 BTSs alongside Britain's railway network.

The term 'mobile' in 'GSM-R' refers to the equipment that will need to be fitted to all driving cabs and to portable handsets that can be used by railway staff. Once the infrastructure for GSM-R has been fitted to the network, and all driving cabs have been equipped, NRN and CSR will no longer be used. At the time of writing a trial of trains fitted with the GSM-R system, in parallel with the existing CSR system, is being conducted in the Strathclyde area.

GSM-R is already in use in areas that have been resignalled using axle counters (*e.g.* much of the route from Euston to Manchester, and in the Bournemouth and Portsmouth areas). However, in such cases the equipment has not been fitted to driving cabs: instead drivers have been issued with GSM-R mobile phones for use in emergencies. This is known as the *Interim Voice Radio System* (IVRS) and has been provided to supplement NRN wherever track-circuit operating clips are no longer of any use to protect the line in an emergency. IVRS provides a robust means of contacting the signaller in an emergency, but eventually, as the trains are equipped with GSM-R, IVRS will cease to be used.

PART 9

Chapter 33   Engineering operations on the line

From time to time the line may become unsafe for various reasons, such as landslip, flooding and washout, or when it is under repair or renewal, and it is necessary to ensure that no train can enter a section of line thus affected. The arrangements for ensuring the safety of trains are of three kinds:

1. Protection when the line is unsafe
2. Protection of engineering work that is not being carried out under an Absolute Possession
3. Protection of engineering work that is being carried out under an Absolute Possession

Protection when the line is unsafe

When the line is unsafe for trains to run on it, three things must be done at once:

1. A track-circuit-operating clip must be placed on the line to place signals to Danger
2. Detonator protection must be provided
3. The signaller must be told as quickly as possible

Detonator protection consists of placing three detonators on the line, 22 yards (20m) apart, 1¼ mile (2km) away. However, in the following circumstances the three detonators must be placed on the line immediately, before reaching that distance:

1. If a train approaches
2. If the person carrying out the duty reaches a signalbox or telephone communicating with a signalbox before then, in which case the detonators need not be placed at the full distance if the signaller advises that protection is being given by signals
3. After switching a signal to Danger by means of a signal post replacement switch
4. Before entering a tunnel. If the 1¼ mile (2km) point falls within the tunnel, the detonators must be placed at the far end of it.
5. Just before a trailing junction. Both legs of the junction must be protected, and it is a

question of judgement as to which is done first.

The person concerned must remain at the detonators showing a red flag or lamp until the line is again safe for trains to pass.

Protection of engineering work not carried out under Absolute Possession

The work should be planned in advance wherever possible, to minimise interference with the running of trains. The person responsible for arranging protection must be qualified to do so, and is known as the *controller of site safety* (COSS). He must make appropriate arrangements with the signaller, and will be given an *authority number*. One of the following protection procedures must be carried out.

1. Place a track-circuit operating device (T-COD) on the track. The signaller must check that the track circuit concerned is initially clear but shows occupied when the T-COD is applied.
2. Disconnect the protecting signal so that it can only show a Stop aspect, but only if competent and certificated to do so.
3. Send out a handsignaller with detonators under arrangements similar to those that apply when the line is unsafe.

These arrangements may also be used to safeguard anyone working on or near the line who may be endangered by passing trains, or when cranes or other mechanical equipment that may foul the line are being used.

Protection of engineering work under Absolute Possession

These arrangements are normally used whenever engineering operations are to be carried out using engineers' trains or on-track machines or plant. There may be several worksites within one possession, which may extend for several miles, although the length of line under possession should be kept to a minimum, as the normal signalling arrangements are suspended. No train other than an engineers' train may pass through a possession.

The arrangements for ensuring safety are detailed and lengthy and fall under the following headings:

1. The appointment of specific people with special responsibilities
2. The protection of the possession
3. Controlling the movement of trains from the 'live' railway into the area of the possession
4. Protection of individual worksites
5. Controlling the movement of trains within the possession
6. Controlling the movement of trains from the possession into the 'live' railway
7. Giving up the possession

The word *train* includes engineers' on-track machines such as tamping machines, ballast regulators etc, whereas other plant such as road/rail vehicles and rail-mounted maintenance machines are known as *possession-only rail vehicles* and are not permitted to work or run outside possessions.

Appointment of specific people

The *person in charge of the possession* (PICOP) must be certified as competent and familiar with the line and the arrangements in force. He must normally have no other responsibilities. He wears an appropriately worded armband.

The engineering supervisor in charge of each worksite wears an appropriately worded armband.

The controller of site safety in charge of each work group in a worksite wears an appropriately worded armband.

Protection of a possession

Protection is provided by fixed signals and by detonators, three of which are positioned 22 yards (20m) apart at both ends of the possession. The detonators in rear of the possession are generally placed ¼ mile (400m) beyond the protecting signal; those at the other end of the possession are generally placed ¼ mile (400m) before a stop signal. A *possession limit board*, consisting of a stop sign and a flashing red light, is placed next to the centre detonator. The protection is intended not only to prevent a train from straying wrongly into the possession but also to prevent a train from straying from inside the possession onto the 'live' railway.

Trains entering a possession

The signaller must not allow a train to proceed towards the protecting detonators from either end without the PICOP's permission. Having obtained his permission, he must tell the driver what is happening and instruct him to pass the protecting signal at Danger and proceed cautiously to the protecting detonators, from which point the PICOP will authorise the next movement.

Protection of individual worksites

Individual worksites must be indicated by marker boards except where there are no engineers' trains or on-track machines within the possession, or where there is only one worksite, and the only movements are on-track machines. The marker boards are double-sided, and have two flashing lights, arranged vertically. Red lights indicate the entrance to the worksite; the board is not to be passed unless the engineering supervisor authorises it. Yellow lights indicate the exit from the worksite; the board is not to be passed without the PICOP's authority. The boards are positioned at least 110 yards (100m) from the end of the worksite.

Movements within a possession

Since the normal signalling arrangements are suspended during a possession, all movements must be authorised verbally. The only people authorised to do so are the PICOP and, within a given worksite, the engineering supervisor. All other movements are authorised by the PICOP. Propelling movements are allowed in special conditions. These aspects of possession arrangements need very careful handling, in view of the variety of movements and hazards that can occur, especially as possessions are customarily carried out at night. Trains may move in either direction, they may be split into one or more sections, they may be propelled, they may be stationary, there may be noisy machinery, and there are likely to be a large number of workers both on the trains and on the track.

Movements leaving a possession

The PICOP must tell the signaller when any movement is ready to leave the possession. Authority for such a movement is then given by the signaller.

Giving up a possession

Giving up a possession is one of the most critical activities, since it is essential to ensure that all trains, machines and equipment have been removed from the possession, that all workers on site are aware that the possession is being given up, and that the line is safe for trains to run on. This is the PICOP's responsibility, and he will receive a written certificate from each engineering supervisor to that effect. He can then tell the signaller that he is ready to give up the possession and remove the protection.

At the time of writing Network Rail is reviewing whether to make fundamental changes to the current arrangements for possessions. This is likely to include eliminating the use of possession limit boards and detonators, with reliance placed on the use of fixed signals supplemented by the use of T-CODs, signalling disconnections etc.

It should be noted that the contents of this chapter are only intended to be a brief summary of the arrangements and do not apply to the new high-speed line from St Pancras International through the Channel Tunnel (High Speed 1), on which different arrangements apply. The arrangements for carrying out emergency protection of the line when it is unsafe are detailed in Rule Book Module G1, 'General safety responsibilities', and the arrangements for protecting engineering work are set out in Modules T2 'Protecting engineering work or a hand trolley on a line not under possession' and T3 'Possession of a line for engineering work'.

PART 10

The signalling system installed on the new line from St Pancras International to and through the Channel Tunnel and on to Paris on the TGV Nord high-speed line is a slightly adapted version of a French system known as the TVM430 (*Transmission-Voie Machine*) system, except in the St Pancras International station area. There are no lineside signals, and the driver is informed of the speed at which he is to travel, or whether he is required to stop, by the display of information in his driving cab. Automatic train protection is an inherent part of the system.

The St Pancras International station area served by High Speed 1 is signalled with lineside colour-light signals, and the French KVB (*Contrôle Vitesse par Balise*) system of automatic train protection has been fitted (note that the platforms used by domestic services to the East Midlands and the north are fitted

with conventional British signalling). The KVB system is fitted as standard throughout the French railway system, including on the approaches to Paris Gare du Nord. Trains on High Speed 1 therefore have to switch from cab signalling under the TVM430 system to lineside signals with KVB as they approach St Pancras International.

Track equipment

TVM430 lines are track-circuited throughout and are divided into 1,500m blocks or sections with, at the end of each block, a marker board consisting of a metal plate painted blue with a yellow horizontal triangle, to provide a reference point for the driver. These are of two types: 'non-passable' and 'passable'. Non-passable markers when closed (this is equivalent to being at Danger) can only be passed on the authority of the signaller, and

Above: A Eurostar train emerging from the southern portal of the North Downs Tunnel on High Speed 1. *D. C. Hall*

Left: The first of three views of lineside markers on High Speed 1, featuring a passable block marker with, lower down the post, a local 'Engineering Zone of Protection' switch. *D. C. Hall*

Above: Another passable block marker. *D. C. Hall*

Left: A non-passable block marker, with an auxiliary signal below. *D. C. Hall*

each is also fitted with an auxiliary signal consisting of two lights, similar a position-light signal. These flash white when the signaller has set a route (an auxiliary route) during abnormal working such as a track-circuit failure ahead. Passable markers are not fitted with the auxiliary signal, and can be passed when closed without the authority of the signaller provided that the train speed does not exceed 35km/h. Information is transmitted to the train by means of coded track circuits via the running rails.

The lineside signals at St Pancras are of the fibre-optic type with posts that can be tilted to facilitate maintenance. They have halogen lamps for both the main and auxiliary aspects in either the base of the signal or in a separate cabinet. The light is fed to the signal heads by means of fibre-optic cables. The heads have been designed to tilt to the ground so that maintenance (such as cleaning the lenses) can be carried out from ground level, avoiding the need for ladders or other access equipment.

Train equipment

Traction units are fitted with antennae that receive coded data, transmitted by the UM31 audio-frequency track circuits, containing information about the state of the line ahead, and an on-board processor calculates the maximum speed at which the train may travel, including a braking curve if a reduction of speed is necessary. The speed of the train is controlled by the driver, but if he exceeds the maximum permitted speed on the cab display, or strays outside the braking curve, the brakes are applied. The principle is similar to that adopted for the Automatic Train Protection system already installed on the Great Western main line and the Chiltern line.

The speed codes received by the train contain information about the current maximum safe speed in the block, the target speed at the end of the block and the target speed at the end of the next block. These can each be of five different values corresponding to a typical deceleration curve (300, 270, 230, 170 and 0km/h).

Train controls

The signalling control system is based on the maintenance of a number of unoccupied 1,500m blocks in front of a train. Braking from 300km/h requires five blocks, and an additional 'buffer' block is provided in case of accidental overrun. At this speed, trains are typically about 10.5km apart, or about three minutes' running time.

High Speed 1 is controlled from Ashford control centre and the Channel Tunnel from Folkestone. There is also a control centre in France at Coquelles, which can take over control of the tunnel if Folkestone is out of action for any reason. The Folkestone control centre has a geographical panel 23m long showing the location of all trains. Automatic Route Setting is employed on a large scale.

Out-of-course working

Temporary speed restrictions can be imposed through the TVM430 system either by the signaller or by maintenance staff using lockable switches

Above: Three-aspect colour-light signals at Skipton, with position-light signals below. *Author*

in signalling-equipment rooms. Speed restriction bands are limited to 80, 170, 220 and 270km/h. Speed restrictions can also be imposed using speed boards and portable KVB beacons.

Engineering possessions are taken by the operation of *engineering zones of protection* (EZP) by the signaller at Ashford control centre. This prevents routes (other than auxiliary routes) into the protected area from being set. Local switches are also operated by the responsible person on site. If the possession is of one line only, the system imposes a speed restriction on the adjacent line.

It should be noted that detonators and track-circuit-operating devices are not used on High Speed 1.

PART 11

Chapter 35   Future developments

The development of signalling technology, both by railway undertakings themselves and by national and international signalling contractors, has been a continuous process, although its application to Britain's railways has been marked by a series of major advances:

1. The application of electric power to the operation of points
2. The introduction of the electrically-lit colour-light signal
3. The invention of the track circuit
4. The replacement of mechanical interlocking by electrical relay interlocking
5. The one control switch (OCS) system of setting a route and clearing signals, allowing one signalbox to control large areas
6. The refinement of the OCS system into the entrance/exit (NX) system, which became the BR standard in the 1960s
7. The application of solid-state computer technology to signalling interlocking, replacing relays
8. The adoption of visual-display units in signalling centre operating rooms, replacing the large indications panels
9. The use of tracker-balls and keyboards, instead of push-buttons on large control panels, for use by the signaller in controlling points and signals
10. The use of radio for vital signalling messages, as in the Radio Electronic Token Block system
11. The application of computers to the automation of route-setting.
12. The implementation of train-protection systems ranging from AWS to TPWS and ATP
13. The use of cab signalling now implemented for trains on High Speed 1, and to be an inherent feature of the European Train Control System, which will eventually be installed throughout the network

The speed at which modern signalling developments are adopted depends on a number of factors, such as the availability of finance, the capital cost of new equipment, the benefits it might provide in greater reliability and reduced maintenance and operating costs, and the need for improved safety levels.

The factors which lead to existing signalling being replaced in more modern form are:

1. Existing equipment becoming life-expired
2. Electrification schemes, which normally entail major resignalling, both for technical reasons and to cater for higher speeds and altered track layouts
3. Changes in traffic patterns and levels, leading to the need either to reduce signalling costs or to cater for increased traffic levels
4. Conurbation area schemes for improved passenger services, frequently promoted by local authorities and Passenger Transport Executives
5. The desire of train operators for higher speeds

As far as main and suburban lines are concerned, the standard that has now been adopted is the Integrated Electronic Control Centre (IECC), incorporating solid-state interlocking, visual-display units and tracker-ball/keyboard for use by the signaller, and Automatic Route Setting (ARS). ARS is now widespread where train services are regular and reliable. It produces a more predictable response and is capable of being programmed to make the optimum decisions in the event of interruptions to the service arising from late running, cancellations and mishaps etc.

The next stage in development is the signalling-control centre replacing the earlier 1960s power signalboxes that used relay technology. Typical examples are the new control centres built at Saltley to control the West Midlands and at Derby to control the East Midlands, their areas of control being expanded over the course of several years as earlier power signalling installations are decommissioned.

There remain several thousand miles of double-track secondary line, much of it still mechanically signalled and worked under the traditional Absolute Block system. Traffic levels do not justify the cost of continuous track-circuiting and colour-light signalling, but Network Rail policy does not include the elimination of mechanical signalboxes and Absolute Block working in the immediate future. Staff have been recruited and trained for mechanical interlocking design, installation and maintenance. An alternative solution would be the use of small local panels operating colour-light signals, in locations where there are a number of points, and the interlocking being performed either by relays or by solid-state equipment. The expense of installing track circuits over long lengths of open line can be avoided by the use of axle counters. Often the major cost in a resignalling scheme is the lineside cabling connecting the equipment to a signalbox and providing communication between one signalbox and another.

As far as the resignalling of secondary lines is concerned, no simple, cheap and efficient substitute for the Absolute Block system has yet been found, but it is entirely possible that ETCS Level 2 or 3 will provide the answer, especially when most trains have been equipped with ETCS for use on other routes. Neither lineside signalboxes and signals nor any form of track-based train detection system would be necessary. Line capacity would be increased, and train working would become more efficient. Here is a challenge for the signalling industry.

A system of train detection is needed, not only as part of the signalling system but also to allow the automation of manned level crossings, most of which are situated on secondary lines. The automation of level crossings must continue, because of the savings in manpower costs. It also leads to improved safety levels, and allows signalling installations to be simplified. The pace of the modernisation of level crossings has slowed in recent years, and can proceed only as quickly as the availability of finance and technical resources (including staff) allow. The latter is likely to be the limiting factor.

Track circuits themselves have now reached the limit of their technical development, and they are not always reliable in the detection of certain types of modern multiple-units under the adverse conditions experienced during the leaf-fall season. The unreliability of track circuits causes train delays, which affects the punctuality and reliability of the train service. Axle counters

are increasingly being installed as an alternative to track circuits, but track circuits have benefits in addition to their main purpose of train detection. Track circuits can:

1. Detect the presence of a train by the use of a track-circuit-operating clip
2. Detect the presence of an obstruction
3. Detect a broken rail in some circumstances
4. Hold points in position

There may prove to be no alternative to the use of track circuits in congested station areas.

Radio can provide an answer in certain cases, but the detection of broken rails in the absence of track circuits is a challenge for the permanent-way engineer. He already has to cope with single-rail track circuits on overhead electrified lines.

A major development in signalling and train control philosophy is now taking place — the European Rail Traffic Management System (ERTMS) incorporating the European Train Control System (ETCS). The European Union requires it to be used on Britain's high-speed lines, but ultimately its use on other lines has the potential to bring cost benefits and improvements in efficiency and safety. ETCS in its more advanced modes does not depend on lineside signals, or on track-based train detection systems, which are very expensive to install and maintain and not entirely free from right-side failures, which cause train delays. However, the development processes are proving more prolonged and difficult than was initially envisaged.

The purpose-built high-speed lines in France used by TGVs — and High Speed 1 from St Pancras International through the Channel Tunnel — have no lineside signals, and all the instructions to drivers are picked up from coded messages in the running rails and displayed on the driver's control desk.

Automatic control of the driving of trains is already in operation on some metro lines in Britain and abroad, but whether such a system would ever be applied to the driving of main-line trains is questionable. A driver is needed for other purposes besides the normal driving of the train, such as:

● Keeping a lookout for workers on the track, and sounding the horn to warn them of the train's approach
● Keeping a lookout and sounding the horn when approaching level crossings

- Keeping a lookout for anything that might hazard trains (his own or others), such as flood damage, bridge damage caused by road vehicles, obstructions on the line (either accidental or deliberate), defective track, and animals on the line
- Being on hand to deal with traction failures
- Working through a section under caution for a whole variety of reasons, such as signalling and track-circuit failures, defective track, vandalism, obstructions, animals on the line, and examination of the line

There is little point in automating the driving of trains unless the cost of the driver can be avoided; and as it seems likely, for the reasons given above, that drivers will continue to be needed for purposes other than normal driving, there is little likelihood of any train operator's incurring heavy expenditure in automating the driving of trains, except perhaps in special situations.

Based, therefore, on the retention of drivers, there was a need to modernise or replace the Automatic Warning System (AWS); and a new system, the Train Protection & Warning System (TPWS), was designed as an overlay to AWS. TPWS initiates an irreversible emergency stop if a train approaches a red signal, a buffer stop or a speed restriction too fast for safety, or passes a signal at Danger. TPWS has been installed at about 40% of signals, at locations where the risk of collision or derailment following a SPAD or excessive speed is particularly high. Its installation at signals was completed by the end of 2002.

TPWS has brought a substantial increase in safety. It was initially regarded as a stopgap until ETCS, which incorporates Automatic Train Protection, could be installed, but that is likely to be several years ahead. Indeed, the increase in safety that ETCS would bring is now considered fairly marginal, and its installation will have to be based on a strong financial case and the availability of funds.

Now that collisions and derailments caused by SPADs and overspeeding have been reduced considerably by the installation of TPWS, the outstanding safety issue is becoming the interaction of trains and road vehicles, not merely at level crossings but also at bridges both under and over the railway and, indeed, from lineside properties. It is not possible to eliminate collisions between road vehicles and trains, but improved front-end protection of trains, incorporating obstruction deflectors, can prevent trains from becoming derailed after a collision with road vehicles. Highway authorities need to become more proactive to prevent the escape of road vehicles from the road on to the railway.

APPENDIX

Regulatory authorities and their functions

The Office of Rail Regulation (ORR) is both the economic and the safety regulator of the main-line railway network. It has now fully absorbed Her Majesty's Railway Inspectorate (HMRI) into its structure following HMRI's transfer to the ORR from the Health & Safety Executive in 2006.

The safety regulator has a number of functions, which include investigating accidents and incidents to see whether and to what extent health and safety law has been breached; issuing certificates to railway operators when it has agreed a statement of their safety management arrangements; carrying out inspections and audits of selected railway activities; issuing guidance on how to comply with the law and taking formal enforcement action. The safety regulator has the power to issue enforcement notices and to carry out the prosecution of offenders. Enforcement notices can require improvements to be carried out to an agreed timescale; or where a serious risk of personal injury is found to exist, an inspector can issue a notice prohibiting the activity.

HMRI's former role in investigating railway accidents, to establish the cause and make recommendations, has been transferred to a new organisation, the Rail Accident Investigation Branch (RAIB). The RAIB was formed as the result of a recommendation arising from the serious train accident at Ladbroke Grove on 5 October 1999. It was also a requirement of a European Directive that the two functions of safety regulation and accident investigation should be dealt with by separate organisations. The RAIB became operational in October 2005, and its sole purpose is to improve the safety of the railways in the UK by investigating railway accidents and making recommendations to avoid a recurrence. The RAIB investigates only accidents involving moving trains or matters arising from the operation of trains. It does not investigate incidents such as slips, trips and falls at stations, the investigation of which remains with the safety regulator.

RAIB has no powers to require its recommendations to be implemented. On completion of an investigation, RAIB addresses its recommendations to the safety regulator, which must consider them and, if they are acceptable, monitor their implementation and report progress back to RAIB. If necessary the safety regulator has the powers described above to require recommendations to be implemented.

The Rail Safety and Standards Board (RSSB) was established in April 2003, taking over the functions of the former Safety and Standards Directorate of Railtrack (itself later supplanted by the Railway Safety Organisation). The RSSB is a not-for-profit company that is owned by the industry itself and exists to further the improvement of safety on Britain's railways. It manages the Railway Group Standards (such as the Rule Book), publishes an annual safety plan, sponsors research and development work, monitors safety performance, supports cross-industry groups dealing with particular safety issues, and represents the UK railway industry on European matters.

Technical terms and abbreviations

Absolute Block — A signalling system which allows only one train to be between two signalboxes on the same line at the same time.

Acceptance — A term used in Absolute Block signalling when a signalman allows a train to proceed towards his signalbox.

Accommodation level crossing — A private level crossing connecting land separated by the railway.

Advance — Further along in the direction of travel.

Annunciator — A buzzer which sounds when a train occupies a berth track circuit with the home signal at Danger.

Approach control — A colour-light junction signal which is held at red although the line ahead may be clear, in order to ensure that the driver slows down for a speed-restricted turnout.

Approach locking — A system of locking facing points so that they cannot be moved across in front of an approaching train.

Approach release — The point at which an approach-controlled signal is released.

Aspect — The colour displayed by a colour-light signal.

Automatic barrier crossing (ABCL) — A level crossing whose operation is monitored by the train driver.

Automatic half-barrier crossing (AHB) — An automatically-operated level crossing.

Automatic open crossing (AOCL) — A level crossing without barriers whose road traffic signals are monitored by the driver.

Automatic Route Setting (ARS) — A computerised system for setting routes according to a pre-programmed formula.

Automatic section — An automatically signalled section on an Absolute Block line.

Automatic signal — A signal which is operated by the passage of trains.

Automatic Train Control (ATC) — A former safety device for warning a driver of the need to slow down or stop.

Automatic Train Protection (ATP) — A safety system for ensuring that the driver slows down or stops when necessary.

Automatic Warning System (AWS) — A safety device for warning a driver to slow down or stop.

Axle counters — Track-mounted equipment which counts the number of axles on a train.

Back board — Drivers' name for a distant signal.

Banner repeating signal — A signal which gives a driver advance information about a signal which has a limited sighting distance.

Berth track circuit — Track circuit in rear of home signal.

Block bell — The bell used for sending bell codes between adjacent manual signalboxes.

Block indicator — An instrument indicating the state of the line between adjacent manual signalboxes.

Blocking back — Term used in Absolute Block when an unsignalled train or shunting movement is to be allowed to stand within the clearing point or outside the home signal.

Block section — In Absolute Block, the section of line between the section signal of one signalbox and the home signal of the next signalbox ahead.

Block signalling — A system of signalling based on block sections.

Block switch — Enables a signalbox to be closed by putting the signalboxes on each side into through communication with each other.

Block telephone — A telephone link between two adjacent manual signalboxes, using the block telegraph wires.

Braking distance — The distance a train needs in which to stop.

Bridge bashing — Overheight road vehicles colliding with railway bridges over the road.

Cab Secure Radio (CSR) — A secure form of communication between driver and signaller, and **vice versa**.

Calling-on signal — To allow a train into an occupied section.

Cat's eyes — A railwayman's term for the Proceed aspect of a position light signal.

Classification of trains — A list of the different categories of train.

Clear signal — A colour light signal displaying a green aspect, or a semaphore stop signal in the 'off' position.

Clearing a signal — The action of the signalman in changing a signal from Danger to a Proceed aspect.

Clearing point — The point to which the line must be clear before a train can be accepted from the signalbox in rear under the Absolute Block system of signalling.

Closed-circuit television (CCTV) — Equipment used for remote monitoring or supervisory purposes.

Coaching stock — Vehicles designed to be capable of running in passenger trains.

Colour-light area — An area in which all signals are of the colour light type and usually worked under the Track Circuit Block system.

Colour-light signal — A signal which conveys its message by means of coloured lights.

Controlled signal — A colour light signal which is cleared from red by the signalman.

Cut-out sign — Metal cut-out numerals erected at the lineside to denote the permitted speed.

Delayed yellow — Allows a train to enter a colour light section without the full overlap being available.

Detection — A means of ensuring that facing points are correctly closed before the signal can be cleared.

Detonators — Small disc-shaped warning devices, placed on the rail head, which explode when a train passes over them.

Distant arm proving — A means of ensuring that the distant signal arm is in the 'on' position before the block indicator can be placed to 'Line clear'.

Distant signal — A signal which tells the driver whether he needs to be prepared to stop at the next signal.

Double-yellow aspect — A preliminary caution signal in four-aspect colour light signalling.

Down — All running lines and trains are assigned a direction, either up or down. The up direction is usually towards London or a main centre. Trains using lines which are signalled for both directions are either up or down, according to their individual direction.

Driver's Reminder Appliance — A device in the driving cab which enables the driver to set a reminder that the signal ahead is at Danger.

Electric Token Block — A system of signalling used on single lines.

Electronic token — Used in Radio Electronic Token Block.

Emergency indicator — A sign used to inform a driver of a speed restriction imposed without prior notice.

Emergency replacement switch (ERS) — A switch that enables a signalman to replace an automatic signal to Danger in an emergency.

Enhanced permissible speed (EPS) — increased line speed, applicable to tilting trains; lineside signs are provided

Entrance/Exit system (NX) — A system of route-setting used in modern power signalboxes.

ERTMS — European Railway Train Management System (see Chapter 22).

ETCS — European Train Control System (see Chapter 22).

Examination of line — A method of establishing whether it is safe to run trains through a section.

Facing point — A point which can change the direction of a train approaching it.

Facing-point lock — Equipment for ensuring that facing points cannot move irregularly.

Fail-safe — Signalling equipment is designed so that any failures will result in signals being set at Danger, hence 'fail-safe'.

Fast line — Where there are four separate tracks, one pair of Up and Down lines may be called the Fast lines and the other pair the Slow lines.

Fixed signal — A signal in a fixed location; the word 'fixed' refers to the location and not to the aspect or indication of the signal.

Flank protection — Additional signal and point interlocking at junctions, for extra safety.

Flashing yellow aspects — Warn the driver that he is routed over a speed-restricted turnout at a junction ahead.

Fouling bar — Equipment used to establish that a vehicle is safely clear of the fouling point.

Fouling point — The precise spot where a vehicle standing at a converging point between two lines will come into contact with a vehicle on the other line.

Four-aspect territory — An area where all signals can display four aspects (red, one yellow, two yellows, or green).

Four-foot — Railway term for the space between the two running rails of a line.

Goods line — A line which is not signalled and equipped to the standard needed for passenger trains.

Green aspect — Means that the line ahead is clear and that the next signal will not be at red (or at single yellow in four-aspect territory).

Ground frame — A stage or cabin containing switches or levers for controlling points and signals, but which can only be used when released by the controlling signalbox.

GSM-R — Global System for Mobile Communication — Railway (see Chapter 32).

Half-cock — Term used by drivers to describe a semaphore signal that is halfway between 'on' and 'off'.

Handshake — Simultaneous successful operation of separate electronic devices in the same system.

Handsignalman — Person stationed at the lineside to give signals to the driver by flag or lamp.

Headway — The minimum distance between two trains travelling in the same direction that will enable green signals to be given to the driver of the second train and enable him to travel at unrestricted speed.

Home normal contact (HNC) — A means of ensuring that the home signal lever is replaced in the frame before 'Line clear' can be given.

Home signal — In Absolute Block, the first (or outermost) stop signal on the approach to a signalbox. May also be called 'outer home' or 'home No 1' where there are two home signals.

Hot-axlebox detector (HABD) — Apparatus for detecting an overheated axlebox on a rail vehicle.

Hudd system of ATC — A former system of warning the driver of the need to slow down or stop.

Illuminated diagram — A panel in a signalbox containing a diagrammatic representation of the track under the signalman's control and with certain functions, such as the location of trains, being shown by lights.

Integrated Electronic Control Centre (IECC) — The most modern type of signalbox, with visual-display units instead of control panels, and with routes being set by tracker-ball or keyboard instead of push-button. They have solid-state interlocking controls and Automatic Route Setting.

Interim Voice radio system (IVRS) — Used to supplement the National Radio Network in some areas

Intermediate Block Section (IBS) — An additional unstaffed block section between two Absolute Block signalboxes, generally worked from the rear signalbox.

Isolate — Take equipment out of use.

Junction indicator — Displayed at a junction signal to inform the driver which way a junction is set.

King lever — A lever whose operation unlocks other levers.

Lamp proving — A system of ensuring that a lamp in a colour light signal is lit before the next signal in rear can show a Proceed aspect.

Lever collar — Piece of equipment placed over a lever to prevent it from physically being moved.

Light-emitting diode (LED) — Provides a tiny bright light when illuminated.

Line — A loose term which can mean just one pair of rails, e.g. the up line, or all the tracks on a route.

Line clear — The position of the block indicator when a signalman has accepted a train.

Line speed — The maximum permitted speed of a line.

Main aspect — The red, yellow, double-yellow or green aspect of a colour-light signal.

Manually controlled barriers (MCB) — A manned level crossing with barriers.

Manual signalbox — A signalbox in which the signal- and points-operating levers are pulled over and replaced by physical effort.

Miniature warning lights (MWL) — Small red and green lights at certain types of level crossing.

Multiple-aspect signal — A colour light signal capable of displaying three or four aspects.

National Radio Network (NRN) — A radio system providing a link between driver and signaller, and between the signaller and staff working on the line.

Nearside — The left-hand side in the direction of travel.

Normal — Denotes the usual position in which points lie.

No Signaller Token System (NST) — A method of working trains over a single line with a signalman at only one end of the section.

NX system — See **Entrance/Exit system**.

Occupation level crossing — A private level crossing, usually giving access between premises and a public road.

Occupied — Denotes the presence of a train.

Off — A Proceed aspect in a colour light signal, or a semaphore signal arm inclined at 45°.

Offside — The right-hand side in the direction of travel.

On — A red aspect in a colour light signal, or a semaphore signal arm in the horizontal position.

One-control switch system (OCS) — A route-setting signalling system in which a point and the junction signal are set by turning the appropriate switch.

One-train working (OTW) — A method of working a single line by confining it to one train at a time.

Open level crossing — An unmanned crossing without road traffic signals.

Out of correspondence — Denotes that points are not correctly set.

Overlap — A section of line beyond a signal which, for safety reasons, must be clear before the next signal in rear can show a Proceed aspect.

Overspeed sensor —That part of the TPWS system which checks whether the driver is responding appropriately to a Caution signal.

Passenger line — One signalled and equipped for use by passenger trains.

Permanent speed restriction (PSR) — A restriction imposed owing to sharp curves or other permanent cause.

Permissive Block system — A signalling system which allows more than one train to be in a section on the same line at the same time.

PICOP — Person in charge of possession (during engineering work etc).

Pilotman — A person appointed to conduct trains over a single line or a line being used for trains in both directions, during failure of equipment or repairs, or owing to an obstruction.

Platform starting signal — A stop signal at the departure end of a passenger station platform.

Position-light ground signal (PLGS) — A signal on the ground, controlling shunting movements.

Position-light signal (PLS) — A signal located on the same post as a colour light running signal, and fixed below it. It controls train movements other than normal running movements.

Power signalbox (PSB) — A signalbox in which points and signals are operated by electric or other power and controlled by switch or push-button. Interlocking between points and signals is performed by electric relays. PSBs usually cover large areas, and have large control and indications panels.

Preliminary Route Indicator (PRI) — Used in junction signalling.

Proceed aspect — A green, yellow or double-yellow light shown at a colour light signal, which means that the driver may proceed past it.

Protection of the line — Warning action taken to stop trains running into an obstruction, a failed train or other source of danger.

Radio Electronic Token Block (RETB) — A signalling system used on single lines.

Rear — Behind, in the direction of travel, i.e. a section of line over which a train has already passed.

Red aspect — Danger, stop. Displayed by a colour-light signal.

Reminder appliance — Used in manual signalling to remind a signalman of the presence of a train or other circumstance.

Repeater — A dial or indicator in a manual signalbox, showing the position of a signal arm and whether the signal lamp is lit.

Reverse — Denotes that points are lying in a position opposite to normal.

Rotary block — A special type of block instrument, used in some former Midland Railway signalboxes.

Route-relay interlocking — A system of interlocking between points and signals, performed by electric relays.

Ruling gradient — The main or most important gradient on a section of line with more than one gradient.

Running line — Any line other than a siding. Train movements on running lines are controlled by fixed signals.

Running movement — A normal train movement on a running line, under the control of a running signal.

Running signal — A main aspect in a colour light signal, or a distant or stop semaphore signal.

SASSPAD — Start-against-signal SPAD.

Section signal — In Absolute Block, the most advanced stop signal (i.e. the signal which admits a train to the block section ahead).

Semaphore signal — A fixed signal, whose meaning is given to drivers by the position of an oblong arm during daylight, and by coloured lights at night.

Semi-automatic signal — A colour light signal which is worked automatically by the passage of trains, but which can also be controlled from a signalbox or ground frame.

Sequential locking — Interlocking between signal levers to ensure that they are pulled over in the correct sequence.

Service brake application — The normal brake application which is made by a driver in routine service (as opposed to an emergency application).

Setting back — Denotes a short-distance shunting movement, usually in the wrong direction.

Shunt-ahead signal — Allows a driver to pass a stop signal by a short distance for shunting purposes.

Shunt frame — Similar to a ground frame, but often a former signalbox.

Shunt movement — A short-distance movement, often setting back through points, and controlled by shunting signals.

Sighting distance — The maximum distance at which a driver can see a signal ahead of him.

Signal sighting — The driver's approach view of signals.

Signalling panel — A panel in a signalbox giving a diagrammatic representation of the layout under the signalman's control, together with control switches or push-buttons and track circuit etc indications.

Signalpost replacement switch — A switch at the foot of an automatic colour light signal, which enables the signal to be switched to (and maintained at) red by the use of a key.

Signalpost telephone (SPT) — A telephone provided at a signal for the driver to speak to the signalman.

Six-foot — A term for the space between the up and down lines.

Slack — A term for a temporary speed restriction.

Slotting — A mechanism for controlling semaphore signal arms where two signalboxes are involved.

Slow line — A name often used for one of a pair of lines, e.g. the up slow line, where there are four lines of way (see **Fast line**).

Solid-state interlocking — A computerised software system for controlling the interlocking between points and signals.

SPAD — Signal passed at Danger without authority.

SPAD alarm — Provided in signalling centres and triggered if a driver wrongly passes a signal at Danger.

SPAD signal — A signal which is normally unlit but which flashes when a driver passes a signal at Danger without authority about 50yd in rear.

SPATE indicator — Used in connection with temporary speed restrictions.

Speed indicator — A sign erected at the running-on end of a temporary speed restriction.

Splitting distants — Two distant signals erected side by side, to tell a driver in advance which way he is routed at the junction ahead.

Staff (or train staff) — A form of token used in the working of a single line.

Staff-and-ticket working — An obsolete form of controlling the working of trains over a single line.

Starting signal — See **Section signal**.

Station limits — The section of line between the outermost home signal and the most advanced stop signal worked from the same signalbox.

Station working — Special regulations governing shunting movements within station limits.

Stop signal — A signal capable of showing a stop aspect or indication.

Subsidiary signal — In semaphore signalling, a calling-on or shunt-ahead signal.

Sunflower — Drivers' name for the AWS visual indicator.

Sykes Lock & Block signalling — A former method of signalling.

Temporary speed restriction (TSR) — A speed restriction imposed for a short period.

Termination indicator — A sign at the running-off end of a temporary speed restriction.

Token — A physical object, e.g. a tablet, staff or key, used in the Electric Token Block method of signalling single lines.

Tokenless block — A method of working single lines without using a token.

TPWS — See **Train Protection & Warning System**.

TPWS+ — Provides overspeed protection on higher-speed lines.

Track — A term which loosely includes the rails and sleepers, or generically as in 'track and signalling'.

Track circuit — An electrically-operated train detection device, which uses the running rails.

Track-circuit block (TCB) — A method of working trains over lines which are continuously track-circuited and equipped with multiple-aspect colour light signals.

Track-circuit-operating clip — A safety device carried in driving cabs and guards' vans, which is placed on the track and, by short-circuiting the track circuit, places the signal in rear at red.

Track-circuit-operating device (T-COD) — Used to protect staff working on the line.

Tracker-ball — A means by which the signalman enters his commands and controls points and signals in an IECC.

Traffic moment — A measure of the combined quantity of road and rail traffic at a level crossing.

Trailing points — Points which cannot alter the direction of trains passing through them; when used in the opposite direction they become facing points.

Train describer — Apparatus used in modern signalboxes, which indicates to the signalman the location and identity of trains.

Train description (TD) — A four-character identity number carried by each train.

Train-operated route release (TORR) — A method of cancelling a route automatically after a train has passed over it.

Train Protection & Warning System (TPWS) — Monitors the driver's response to a warning signal and applies the brakes if a signal is passed at Danger.

Train Ready to Start plunger — A means by which station staff inform a signalman that a train is ready to depart.

Train Register Book — A book kept in signalboxes for recording the passage of trains and other events.

Train-stop sensor — That part of the TPWS system which applies the brakes if a signal is passed at Danger.

Transponder — Equipment fixed between the rails which passes information electronically to a train passing over it.

Trap points — A switch blade or blades, which normally lie open to derail any vehicles which might otherwise escape from a goods line or sidings on to a passenger line.

Treadle — A mechanical or electronic device fixed to one of the rails for detecting the passage of a train over it.

TVM430 — French signalling system for high-speed trains; used between London and Paris.

Unbooked route — Not the route shown in the working timetable.

Up — A direction applied to a running line or train (see also **Down**).

Visual-display unit (VDU) — A screen on which various types of information can be displayed.

Warning board — A warning sign to a driver that he is approaching a temporary speed restriction.

'Welwyn' Control — A safety system applied to the operation of the block indicator.

Wheel-impact-load detector — Measures the impact load of each wheel on a train and sounds an alarm if an unacceptable load is detected.

Wire adjusters — Equipment in a signalbox for adjusting the tension in the wire operating a signal.

Wrong direction — A train movement in a direction which is opposite to the normal one.

Wrong-side failure — A failure of signalling equipment which does not place the protecting signal to Danger (see **Fail-safe**).

Yellow aspect — Displayed by a colour-light signal, and warns a driver to expect to find the next signal at red..